As a health professional, Ben ... ss, diagnose and treat. Wonderful ... ...ose skills to not only analyse the cultura ... ...s of the day but also critique the church's response to those movements. The result is a tool that will greatly help us fulfil the Great Commission to our generation.

RICO TICE
Author and Founder of Christianity Explored Ministries

Christian persuaders need more than logical arguments. Since the early Greek rhetoricians, we have known that to make an effective case you need personal credibility and a connection with the emotions as well. The Apostle Paul knew this: he reminded believers that his gospel had come to them 'not simply with words but also with power, with the Holy Spirit and deep conviction. You know how we lived among you for your sake' (I Thess. 1:5). Ben Chang gets this. He understands that paying attention to the broader philosophical and cultural context, as well as ensuring we 'connect' with our listeners at an emotional level, doesn't weaken Gospel proclamation it strengthens it. Today, more than ever, we need courageous 'contenders', able to navigate the pitfalls of cancel culture whilst making arguments that win hearts as well as minds. Ben has produced a bold, insightful and supremely practical primer that will be read by young people's and youth group leaders, students, pastors and evangelists – indeed, anybody – with a heart to bring the light of Christ to a darkening age.

GLYNN HARRISON
Retired Psychiatrist, Emeritus Professor of Psychiatry (Bristol University), Author, *A Better Story: God, Sex and Human Flourishing*

In the confusing kaleidoscopic world of identity politics and culture wars a simple explanatory guide is a real help. In this book Benjamin Chang explains the history of some of the dominant movements that are simultaneously shaping and splitting society around us, and helps us understand the philosophical roots of how we have got to where we are. But where do we go from here? How can we share the Good News in a culture that increasingly rejects Christianity as oppressively bad news? Informed and informative, readable and engaging, this book is a handbook for those who not only want to understand the world around us, but are striving for a more effective missional engagement with it.

CHRIS WRIGHT
Langham Partnership, Author, *The Mission of God's People*

In this thoughtful and timely book, Ben Chang tackles some of the most contentious issues of our time with wisdom, sensitivity and humility. For the sake of the gospel in the west, it is imperative that his invitation to engage with these issues – and more than issues, people – is heeded by all who profess Jesus as Lord. It is vital for a church caught in the crosswinds of cultural change to develop language and hone wisdom to understand the times. I consider this a resource useful to that end.

DAM IIOIA MAKINDE
Advocacy Engagement Lead, Evangelical Alliance

Informative, perceptive, insightful. Ben Chang provides an invaluable and readable resource for all of us, examining the major social justice issues of the 21st century and modelling thoughtful and astute Christian responses. Ben models a gracious, perceptive and nuanced way of engaging with the polarised and toxic debates of the culture wars and identity politics. This is essential reading for all who want to better understand the confusing world we live in and how the Gospel of redemption has fresh relevance.

JOHN WYATT
Emeritus Professor of Ethics and Perinatology (UCL),
Author, *Matters of Life and Death* and *The Robot Will See You Now*

With commendable clarity and brevity, Ben Chang guides the reader through the minefield of identity politics and offers practical and practicable ways to better engage with the critical issues of our day. A must-read for any Christian who not only wants to better understand the issues but also wants to know how to respond in a constructive and Christ-like manner.

MARTIN SALTER
Lead Pastor, Grace Community Church, Bedford,
Author, *So Loved: 26 Words That Can Change Your Life*

Chang has embarked upon a bold project – to show a better way for Bible-believing Christians to understand and engage with our convoluted and complex culture. The book is brief and accessible enough to be clear, yet substantial enough to show nuance and a real understanding of matters. It is well researched, concisely crunched, wise in alternative approaches, measured in self-criticism, all while being tethered to a high view of Scripture. I found this book a great help personally to understanding some of the cultural trends in our generation and I particularly appreciated the constant thread seen throughout the book – a heart for evangelism and dialogue. It is so important in our generation to see those around us not as the enemy, but as our mission. Chang has helped us by giving us a handle on complex matters. Every pastor and thoughtful Christian will be helped by this book.

GRANT RETIEF
Rector, Christ Church Stellenbosch, South Africa

Unlike any other time in history, identity politics is shaping and changing the world that we live in. However, it is precisely here that many Christians get stuck – not knowing how to navigate its complexity, where their beliefs might fit, and how to act in response. In Christ and the Culture Wars, Ben Chang provides a clear framework for understanding how we got to where we are today. He uncovers the power of listening to the stories of the oppressed and sets out a balanced call for Christians to move forward through the transformational narrative of redemption. The book is challenging, succinct, insightful and practical – a vital resource in equipping Christians to think differently about engaging in contemporary cultures.

ABIGAIL MAGUIRE
Head of Undergraduate Studies, Moorlands College

This book is a must for Christians seeking to engage well and reach out to others in a world that increasingly casts Christianity on the wrong side of history. Ben carefully unpacks the origins and evolution of the social justice movements and how they are shaping the cultural landscape in the global west. He looks at how Christians are responding. But, more importantly, he points to how we might tell a better story of redemption and liberation.

KEN WRIGHT
Former Chair, British Youth for Christ

Ben Chang has done us all a service in this clear and simple introduction to one of the most powerful trends in West at the moment. If you are struggling to understand the term 'identity politics', the grip it has on our culture or even how we got here, this is the book for you. However, with a background in medicine, Ben doesn't simply diagnose the condition, he tests possible 'treatments' and shows that the only effective response to this destructive philosophy is a holistic Christian life and witness. Only in the gospel of Jesus Christ – shared in word and deed – can the true identity, justice and hopes of the West be found.

STEPHEN NICHOLS
Vicar, All Saints Church, Lindfield

This book is extremely timely. In a culture that is so divided and filled with warring factions, Ben Chang helps disciples of Jesus think through how to live redemptively and be good witnesses to the gospel. Chang helpfully takes a scalpel to various aspects of modern culture, exploring their historic roots and how they became what we see today. He then takes that same scalpel and analyses how, as believers, we have responded to the culture wars going on around us, highlighting the deficiencies in mirroring, arguing against or ignoring what is happening. Instead, *Christ and the Culture Wars* outlines a gentle challenge to us as followers of Christ to tell a better story – a story of redemption and grace. A great read for anyone who wants to love Jesus and speak for him in a divided world.

MATT HOIDEN
Children and Youth Ministry Leader, Keswick Ministries, UK

In a culture increasingly and passionately polarised around issues of identity, sexuality, equality and justice, Ben Chang gives us a masterful, concise and compelling summary of the history and dynamics of four key movements and a robust analysis of the flaws in the major Christian responses. Chang then goes on to explore a dynamic way forward rooted in the Cross and how it not only addresses and meets the deep yearnings of our culture for identity, equality, justice and freedom but calls Christians to live out the Cross' implications in generous redemptive living. Bravo indeed.

MARK GREENE
Mission Champion, London Institute of Contemporary Christianity

CHRIST AND THE CULTURE WARS

SPEAKING FOR JESUS
IN A WORLD OF IDENTITY POLITICS

BEN CHANG

CHRISTIAN
FOCUS

paperback ISBN 978-1-5271-0976-6
ebook ISBN 978-1-5271-1031-1

10 9 8 7 6 5 4 3 2 1

Published in 2023
by
Christian Focus Publications Ltd,
Geanies House, Fearn, Ross-shire,
IV20 1TW, Great Britain.

www.christianfocus.com

Cover design by
Alister MacInnes (MOOSE77)

Printed and bound by
Bell & Bain, Glasgow

Contents

To my godson Emmanuel

I have no idea what kind of world you are going to grow up in. But whatever happens around you, I pray that you will grow up to know and love Jesus.

Acknowledgements

I'd like to express my deep gratitude to the many people who have helped this book come into being.

I want to thank my wise friends Rhian, Shilpita, Jess and Jubi who read and gave feedback on early drafts. Thanks also to my editor Ruth and the whole team at Christian Focus who have made this book a reality.

In addition there are two individuals who deserve special mention.

Firstly I want to thank Prof. Glynn Harrison who not only inspired and encouraged me to think about these topics and write this book, but also spent a considerable amount of time looking over draft chapters and offering suggestions and amendments. This book would have never happened if it weren't for your friendship and mentoring.

But the biggest thanks of all goes to my fiancé Lara, who was pretty much the first and last person to read every chapter, and who has been enormously patient, supportive, loving and wise throughout this whole book-writing journey. I can't wait to spend the rest of my life with you.

Of course, I retain responsibility for any remaining errors or inaccuracies in this book.

Introduction

'What is this babbler trying to say?'
Athenian philosophers, Acts 17:18

In the Spring of 1954, the American evangelist Billy Graham touched down in the UK for his first Haringey Crusade. Night after night, the thirty-six-year-old packed out Haringey Arena as hundreds of thousands came to hear the good news of Jesus. He preached direct, uncomplicated, biblical messages of sin, salvation and repentance, and in response, thousands of Brits publicly committed to following Jesus. Graham went on to inspire a generation of evangelists and Christian laypeople to boldly hold out the good news of Jesus to a spiritually hungry culture. The harvest was plentiful. Maurice Wood, former bishop of Norwich, once said in an interview: 'When I was Principal of Oak Hill Theological College in 1961 I would ask how many newcomers to the College had come to faith following Billy's crusades and there were never less than 10 per cent.'[1]

However, half a century on, the tectonic plates of culture have shifted. As I write this in 2022, our culture in the UK now typically sees the Church less as an open family of love and

15

acceptance, and more as a fortress of patriarchy and repression. Christian morality is often seen less as a framework for wisdom and purity, and more as a regime of narrow-mindedness and a cover for discrimination. And the gospel of Jesus is seen by many less as good news for all humanity, and more as the bigoted edicts of a bygone era.

Furthermore, today's culture is now defined by words and phrases that would have been a foreign language to the young Billy Graham. We live in times marked by 'cancel culture,' 'social justice campaigns,' 'intersectionality' and the 'culture wars.' (We will be returning to all these terms later on and a glossary can also be found at the end of the book for reference). In short, we live in a world shaped by 'identity politics.'

Identity politics is the modern phenomenon by which people have begun to move away from the traditional political divisions of 'left versus right wing,' or 'conservative versus liberal,' and have begun instead to coalesce around identity groups, such as race, sexuality, gender and age. These identity groups have gone on to form the foundations of 'social justice movements' that have radically altered the face of our society in the span of a few years. They have done this, in part, through the telling of a united, powerful and universalisable cultural narrative of the oppressed identity groups waking up to their oppression, and then rising up to overthrow their societal oppressors.

But Christians have found themselves on the wrong side of this cultural revolution. In this cultural story, the Church in general, and the Evangelical Church in particular, is on the side of the oppressors. Christian faith is viewed not as a harmless personal life-choice, or unintellectual fairy tale for the naïve, but as a bastion of oppression that needs to be deconstructed and overthrown.

So what now for evangelism? How can we speak for Jesus in this new and thorny world of identity politics?

The Terrain Ahead

Part 1 of this book explores the stories of the revolution. In Chapters 1-4, we will trace the stories of four of the biggest social justice movements: feminism, racial justice, gay pride and the trans rights movement. We will see how all of these movements began with campaigns for legal equality and against discrimination. But, in recent years, these movements have started calling for broader and more wide-reaching change, sometimes culminating in the overturning of society as we know it. In Chapter 5, we will then pull the strands together to look at the grand over-arching narrative of identity politics. Although all these movements are diverse and sometimes conflicting, they are all united by the overarching story of the oppressed groups rising up to fight against their societal oppressors. However, in this grand narrative Christians have found themselves labelled as the oppressors: the villains of the plotline who need to be overthrown.

In Part 2, we will unpack three common Christian responses to being labelled as the oppressors in the identity politics narrative: mirror, argue and ignore. In Chapter 6 we will see that some (typically white, middle-class, conservative) Christians have tried to *mirror* the identity politics movements, by hunkering down into their own identity groups and fighting for their own rights and liberties that they perceive to be under attack. This has undoubtably contributed to the polarisation of public political discourse and the rise of the so-called 'culture wars.' In Chapter 7 we will see how some Christians have sought to *argue* with and debate the ideas and ideologies of identity politics. After all, there are many legitimate debates to be had, for example: 'are puberty blockers safe to be given to children?' or 'is positive discrimination really fair?' However, debaters soon run into so-called 'cancel culture,' in which those holding 'politically incorrect' views risk being de-platformed, blocked on Twitter, labelled as a bigot and then ignored. Then in Chapter 8, we will explore what seems to be the most common Christian response to the identity politics revolution: just *ignore* it. Many Christians simply bury their heads in the sand, whilst their churches continue running the same events and preaching the same Billy Graham-style evangelistic sermons that they have been doing for decades. It is becoming increasingly recognised however, that our traditional evangelistic messages are not landing like they used to. We cannot keep on ignoring the revolution happening around us.

Part 3 begins to sketch out a possible better way to speak for Jesus in this world of identity politics. In Chapters 9 and 10 we will look at the power of storytelling and consider whether we can re-capture hearts in our culture by telling a more powerful counter-narrative. This may not be as difficult as it appears, because, as we will explore in these chapters, many of the ideas and principles that drive identity politics have deeply Christian historic foundations. In Chapter 11, we will dive deeper into the message of the cross to look at the language we ought to use when preaching salvation in a world of identity politics. We will see that the gospel resonates with a culture when it speaks the language of the culture, and so perhaps we need to re-think how our language frames the good news of Jesus. Finally, in Chapter 12, we will explore how we should *live* as Christians in a world of identity politics. Throughout the biblical narrative, God's people are commanded to live out their redemption, by living redemptively towards others. Today, this may be one of the least discussed parts of Christian living, and yet it seems to be what our culture urgently needs. Our society needs a Church that can not only speak of a redemptive gospel, but live it too.

The topics ahead of us are vast and complex, and so in this relatively short book, there will be many stones left unturned and depths left unexplored. This book is far from a comprehensive sociological analysis of identity politics, or a systematic theology of evangelism and apologetics. Rather, I hope that the following pages act as an interesting introduction that whets appetites and inspires Christians to read and think more about what is happening in our modern culture, and how to speak into it for Jesus.

The Call to Double Listening

Throughout this book we will be trying to engage in what theologian John Stott calls 'double listening.' In *The Contemporary Christian,* Stott implores his readers to listen vigilantly and earnestly to the modern world in all its depth and complexity, and also to listen humbly, submissively and carefully to the Word of God.[2] As Stott concludes, it is only when we have done both that we can then start building a bridge from the Word to the world.[2]

Throughout this book, we will endeavour to do just that. We will be listening intently to what is happening in our culture, as we traverse the worlds of politics, social media, activism, entertainment, education, law, and healthcare, to name just a few. And we will be diving reasonably deeply into the philosophies, ideologies and histories that have fuelled the identity politics movements. But most importantly, we shall be trying to listen carefully and humbly to the Bible, taking it as God's inerrant and authoritative Word that should shape and challenge our minds, hearts and lives. Furthermore, we will be seeking to submit to the Bible as the ultimate grand narrative of reality into which all our stories fit.

Before We Go On...

If it hasn't become apparent already, I am writing this book as a Christian who believes that the gospel is, in the words of the angel at the birth of Jesus, 'good news that will cause great joy for all the people' (Luke 2:10). I also write from the theological position of generally holding to a traditional biblical view on ethical matters, some of which we will be touching on in the following chapters. The purpose of this book is not to give a thorough defence of the authority of Scripture, nor to build detailed cases in favour of the traditional biblical views on particular ethical issues. This book is also not primarily intended to be a thesis on what the 'Christian view' should be on all of the policies and campaigns of the social justice movements. Rather our discussion will be largely focussed on exploring what is going on in our culture and how Christians can bring the good news of the gospel to those around us.

My guess is that most readers of this book will be Christian. However, I do not assume all will be, and I certainly do not assume that all will agree with my positions on the various topics we will be exploring. But whatever your background, I would like to begin by asking for grace. The topics in the following chapters are controversial, sensitive and sometimes explosive. Moreover, there will inevitably be some readers who have been personally affected by subjects covered in this book. These issues are not theoretical concepts to toss around the philosophers' playground; they are personal, practical, and sometimes painful struggles that require compassion before critique. In the pages that follow, I have tried my utmost to be as sensitive, careful, objective and balanced as possible. But where I may have fallen short, I unreservedly ask for grace and forgiveness.

So with some trepidation, let us begin our journey by looking first at the stories of the identity politics revolution.

Part 1:
The Stories of the Revolution

1. Feminism

'Being a woman is a bit tricky... It's not all cake and jam'
Germaine Greer, Women and Power: The Lessons of the 20th
Century (lecture)

*'If all the women who have been sexually harassed or assaulted wrote
"Me too" as a status, we might give people a sense of the magnitude of
the problem'*
Alyssa Milano, on Twitter

In the first Part of this book, we are going to be exploring four of
the largest social justice movements in the world today: feminism,
racial justice, gay pride and the trans rights movement. In each
chapter, we will be taking a brief dive into the historical roots
of the movements, before then exploring more recent events
that have shaped the landscape of modern society. My purpose
in these four chapters is not to give much by way of comment
or critique of these movements. Rather, it is simply to set the
scene and listen to the stories of the cultural revolution, from
the mouths of the protagonists as much as possible. (For this

reason, we may encounter some language that is slightly more colourful than what you may normally expect from a Christian book!) In the interests of relative brevity, we are also going to be focusing mainly on events in the UK and USA, although we will be making occasional trips to some other places along the way. Chapter 5 will then pull the threads together to explore the grand overarching narratives of these social justice movements.

This structure, of dedicating a full five chapters to listening to the stories of our modern culture, is intentional. John Stott once wrote:

> The contemporary world is positively reverberating with cries of anger, frustration and pain. Too often however, we turn a deaf ear to these anguished voices… Our evangelical habit with such is to rush in with the gospel, to climb onto our soapbox, and to declaim our message with little regard for the cultural situation or felt needs of the people concerned.[1]

Stott originally wrote this about thirty years ago. However, it could have easily been written today, about the plethora of Christian books, talks, blogs and podcasts on identity politics that too often rush to the soapbox without carefully and humbly listening to the complexity of voices coming from our modern world.

In this vein, Part 1 of this book tries to listen without speaking, as we explore the stories of the identity politics revolution. And so, we begin with the story of feminism and the fight for women's rights.

The Suffragettes and the Birth of Feminism

The feminist movement is generally seen as starting around the mid-nineteenth century, with what is often referred to as 'First Wave Feminism.' Of course at this point, the desire for equality between men and women was not new. Foundations were laid by female writers in the seventeenth and eighteenth centuries, such as Mary Astell who wrote several books arguing for the need for girls to receive an education equal to boys,' and Marion Reid who contended that women were as rational and moral as men.

However, it was in the mid-nineteenth century that a recognisable feminist movement began to emerge. In the 1850s, Barbara Leigh Smith and a group of her friends began regularly meeting in central London to discuss and organise campaigns for women's rights. Central to their goals was the right to vote. The group became known as the 'Langham Place Group,' named after their early meeting place, and in 1866 they organised the first major suffrage petition which gathered around 1,500 signatures. The petition was handed to their parliamentarian ally John Stuart Mill who presented it to the UK parliament. However, it was voted down by a sizeable majority of Members of Parliament.

In October 1866, Leigh Smith and others set up a suffrage committee in London, which, one year later, became known at the London Society for Women's Suffrage. Soon pro-suffrage groups had formed in multiple cities across the UK. Petition after petition was submitted to parliament, and throughout the 1870s, there were multiple parliamentary votes on women's suffrage. But each one ended in defeat.

At the turn of the twentieth century, however, things started to change. In 1903, Richard and Emmeline Pankhurst, along with their children Christabel and Sylvia, founded the Women's Social and Political Union (WSPU): an organisation that quickly became one of the most publicly recognised and influential groups fighting for women's suffrage. The WSPU's campaigns began with peaceful processions, demonstrations and heckling of political speeches. But gradually, their activism became more direct and dramatic, and soon shop windows were being smashed and post boxes torched. In February 1914, the Northfield Library in Birmingham was burnt to the ground and its contents destroyed. Police were never able to identify the arsonists. However, a book by Christabel Pankhurst was found near the scene, and with it, a note which read 'to start your new library.' In March of that same year, Mary Richardson, who was a leading figure in the WSPU, slashed Velazquez's painting 'Rokeby Venus' in the National Gallery, declaring 'I have tried to destroy the picture of the most beautiful woman in mythological history as a protest against the Government for destroying Mrs Pankhurst, who is the most beautiful character in modern history.'[2]

This period also saw the first well-known martyr for women's suffrage. In 1913, Emily Davidson, who was also a member of the WSPU, travelled to Epsom in Surrey to attend the horse-racing Derby. As the horses headed to the home straight, Davidson ducked under the guard rail and ran onto the course holding a suffrage flag. She threw herself in front of King George V's horse, bringing the horse and rider to the ground in front of multiple cameras and the King and Queen in the audience. Davidson was knocked to the ground unconscious and she died in hospital from a fractured skull a few days later.

Finally in 1918, at the close of the First World War, women over the age of thirty who met a property qualification were granted the vote, and in 1928, the vote was won on equal terms with men.

Equal Pay and Reproductive Rights

Following the end of the Second World War, the feminist movement shifted its focus, becoming what is generally known as 'Second Wave Feminism.' The war itself had given feminism renewed momentum by drawing women into a range of war-time industries and roles that had previously been occupied exclusively by men. One of the most influential figures around this time was the French writer Simone de Beauvoir. In her 1949 book *The Second Sex,* de Beauvoir argues that throughout human history, men have been seen at the archetypal human, whilst women have been seen as the perpetual atypical 'other.' To quote de Beauvoir:

> Woman has ovaries, a uterus; these peculiarities imprison her in her subjectivity, [and] circumscribe her within the limits of her own nature. It is often said that she thinks with her glands. Man superbly ignores the fact that his anatomy also includes glands... He thinks of his body as a direct and normal connection with the world, which he believes he apprehends objectively, whereas he regards the body of woman as a hindrance, a prison, weighed down by everything peculiar to it.[3]

De Beauvoir broadened the goals of feminism from the fight for legal and political rights, to the transformation of how women generally, and women's bodies in particular, were viewed by society. Several other feminist writers followed in de Beauvoir's wake, similarly arguing for the need for society-wide transformation. Germaine Greer's *The Female Eunuch* challenges women's 'sense of inferiority or natural dependence,'[4] whilst Shulamith Firestone, in *The Dialectic of Sex,* proposes a feminist revolution involving 'an analysis of the dynamics of sex war as comprehensive as the Marx-Engels analysis of class antagonism was for the economic revolution.'[5]

One key issue as the heart of Second Wave Feminism was equal pay. Although several campaigners had raised the issue through the period of First Wave Feminism, it was only in the 1960s and 70s that things began to change. In 1968, a large group of female sewing machinists working at the Ford Motor Company's plant in Dagenham went on a strike to protest the fact that they were being paid around 15 percent less than their male colleagues for doing the same work. The strike gained the support of the then Secretary of State for Employment and Productivity Barbara Castle, and in 1970, the Equal Pay Act was passed in parliament, which legally mandated employers to pay employees equal pay for equal work.

But if there was one issue that Second Wave Feminism became known for above all others, it was the issue of reproductive rights.

Birth control became a key matter that epitomised women's right to prioritise and enjoy their sexuality, rather than being the sexual objects of men. In 1916, activist and nurse Margaret Sanger opened the first birth control clinic in the US. However, Sanger was soon arrested for illegally distributing materials on contraception. Spurred on by her friend Sanger, Marie Stopes then opened a similarly pioneering birth control clinic in London, where married women were offered services free of charge. For Second Wave campaigners likes Sanger and Stopes, women's rights were intrinsically tied up with the freedom to sexual enjoyment without the burden of motherhood.

Then, in the 1930s, several key campaigners, turned their attention to the issue of abortion. In the UK, the 1861 Offences Against the Person Act forbade the use of 'poison or other noxious thing, or... use [of] any instrument or other means whatsoever... with intent to procure the miscarriage of any woman.' In 1936, a group of campaigners including writers Janet Chance and Alice Jenkins founded the Abortion Law Reform Association, which became one of the leading organisations campaigning for the legalisation of abortion. Another one of the co-founders and leaders of the Abortion Law Reform Association was Stella Browne who toured England imploring women to take their reproductive rights into their own hands by joining the campaign for the legalisation of abortion. This argument, which focussed on women's personal autonomy, proved powerful. In 1967, the Abortion Act was passed by parliament, which, whilst it did not totally de-criminalise abortions, did now permit abortions on a range of grounds including risk to the physical or mental health of the mother providing the pregnancy is less than twenty-four weeks gestation.

Into the Present

With this brief and admittedly over-simplified summary of the historical roots of feminism in place, we now turn to the feminist movement of the modern era. Some people use the terms 'Third Wave' and 'Fourth Wave' Feminism to categorise the feminist movements of modern times. However, there is a bit of debate around when and where these waves exactly begin and end. I shall leave this debate to others. Rather, our purpose for the remainder of this chapter is to listen carefully to the stories and narratives from the modern feminist movement.

Over the last few decades feminism has seen a rapid evolution. Until fairly recently, the feminist movement had been largely focussed on legislative change, such as for suffrage, equal pay and reproductive rights. However, today's feminist movement has bigger and broader goals. The focus has moved from these specific issues of women's rights, to the structures and systems that are held to stand behind them. And so, the end goal of campaigns is less about parliamentary votes, and more about the widespread reform of society and the deconstruction of the structures and systems that privilege men and oppress women, which is summarised by the now fairly ubiquitous exhortation: 'smash the patriarchy!.'

The Fight for Equity

As we saw earlier in this chapter the Equal Pay Act (1970) legally mandated equal pay for equal work in the UK. In 2010 this Act was then superseded by the broader Equality Act which prohibits discrimination on grounds of sex, as well as age, disability, gender reassignment, marriage or civil partnership, race, religion or belief, and sexual orientation.

The Equal Pay Act and the Equality Act enshrine equal pay for equal work in UK law, and have undoubtably brought greater labour equality between men and women. Nonetheless, the campaign for labour equality did not end with the passing of the

Equality Act. In recent years, feminist activism has shifted away from campaigning for legal reform and equal pay for equal work, and towards the broader fight for 'equality of outcomes'- the endeavour to ensure that the markers of success and achievement are equally distributed between men and women. This equal distribution of outcomes is sometimes referred to as 'equity.'

Despite the institution of the Equality Act there is still a persisting and often-quoted gender pay gap in the UK. The Office of National Statistics defines the gender pay gap as the difference in average hourly earnings between men and women (excluding overtime), and reported it to be 15.4 per cent in 2021, up from 14.9 per cent the previous year.[6] The government's Gender Equality Monitor report published in 2019 also found that unemployment was 8.9 per cent higher in women than in men, and just 26.7 per cent of FTSE 350 company board members were women.[7]

This notable ongoing inequity between men and women has led to campaigns to level the playing field through the establishment of what is known as 'positive discrimination' in the UK, or 'affirmative action' in the US. Positive discrimination is where organisations ensure equal or comparable outcomes between men and women, through the deployment of quotas and/or requirements that advantage women (as well as other minorities, as we shall explore in the next chapter). As the writer and founder of the Everyday Sexism Project Laura Bates argues, positive discrimination is necessary 'in situations where discrimination already exists- in the form of a system of unofficial, normalised inequality which we have come to accept as "just the way things are"...These measures [are] correcting existing inequality rather than creating it.'[8] Bates argues that society is built in a way that fundamentally and systematically disadvantages women, and so to reach true equality, we must put in place structures that systematically advantage women, so as to compensate for these structural biases.

Resulting from a range of campaigns, there are now many organisations and institutions in the UK and globally that utilise positive discrimination in some form. One of the most significant is the UK Labour Party. In the 1980s and early 90s, less than 10 per cent of UK MPs were women. In an attempt to increase the representation of women in parliament, for the 1997 election, the Labour Party introduced all-women shortlists for half of their winnable seats. One of these women who was elected from an all-women shortlist in 1997 was Jacqui Smith, who eventually became the first female UK Home Secretary.

However, the introduction of all-women shortlists was far from uncontroversial. One local Labour party refused to comply, and two male politicians who were prevented from standing for election because of the all-women shortlists challenged the policy in court, on the grounds that they were being discriminated against because of their gender. Nonetheless, all-women shortlists have remained Labour policy, and in the 2019 election, Labour reached the mark of having over 50 per cent of their elected MPs being women.

The Labour Party is just one of several examples we could give of organisations adopting positive discrimination. In some ways, winning equal pay for equal work was the beginning, rather than the end, of the fight for labour equality. Rather than settling for legal equality as laid out by the Equal Pay Act, campaigners for positive discrimination are now clear that their aim is equality of outcomes between men and women, and one of the main routes to achieving this goal is through the systematic advantaging of women, to compensate for the structural biases against them.

What to Wear

But equality is not just about money or statistics. In 2011, police constable Michael Sanguinetti, along with his colleague, was invited to give a presentation to a small group of law students at York University, Toronto, on the topic of campus safety.

However, the event panned out in a way that nobody could have predicted.

As his colleague was speaking, Sanguinetti chose to interrupt and announced: 'I've been told I'm not supposed to say this- however, women should avoid dressing like sluts in order not to be victimised.' The remark sparked widespread fury and hit international headlines. It also inspired the movement of so-called 'SlutWalk' protests. The first of these 'Slutwalks' drew thousands of protesters to Queen's Park, Toronto, with many wearing revealing or minimal clothing. Within a few months, the movement had gone global. Similar protests were organised across the USA, Australia, New Zealand and the UK, and continued long after Sanguinetti publicly apologised for his remarks and was disciplined by his department. The organisers of the first London 'SlutWalk' in October 2011 explained the reason for the protest on their website:

> All over the world, women are constantly made to feel like victims, told they should not look a certain way… should not wear high heels or make-up… Not only does this divert attention away from the real cause of the crime- the perpetrator- but it creates a culture where rape is OK, where it's allowed to happen.[9]

The message from the protests was clear – women should have the right to dress how they like, including baring as much skin as they like, without them being fearful of unwanted sexual advances. Writer Jessica Valenti described these protests in *The Washington Post* as the 'most successful feminist action of the past 20 years… SlutWalks stand out as a reminder of feminism's more grass-roots past and point to what the future could look like.'[10]

This principle played out in a more recent US television moment that has been viewed over 2 million times on YouTube. In 2016, actress Mayim Bialik (who played Amy Farrah Fowler in *The Big Bang Theory*) and TV presenter Piers Morgan appeared on *The Late Late Show* with James Corden. With Bialik and Morgan sitting side-by-side on Corden's guests' couch, Corden asked Morgan about a controversy he had been involved in, referred to as '#cleavagegate.' Morgan explained that it had started with a negative comment Morgan made on social media in response to the actress Susan Sarandon wearing a low-cut top whilst presenting the in-memoriam section of the Screen Actors Guild Awards that year. Morgan reiterated his belief to Cordon that he felt it was slightly inappropriate for Sarandon to wear such an outfit whilst paying tribute to actors and actresses who had passed away the previous year.

But before Morgan could go on, Mayim Bialik reached across, grabbed Morgan's wrist and said: 'you know what, I identify as a feminist. I'm going to do it this way.' She then stood up, faced Morgan with her back to the camera, and opened up the front of her dress, showing her cleavage to a startled Morgan. Corden, Morgan and the TV audience erupted in laughter, and Morgan was left visibly blushing.

In some ways, the protesters that took to Queen's Park in 2016, and Mayim Bialik exposing her cleavage to Piers Morgan, were proclaiming the same message: in a society where many women live in persistent fear of unwanted sexual comments, advances and assault, women are empowered when they stand up for their right to wear what they like and to bare as much skin as they like. Furthermore, to suggest that a women should dress more modestly would be an act of misogyny.

#MeToo

Of course tragically, for many women, these fears of unwanted sexual advances are far from theoretical.

Up until 2017, film director and producer Harvey Weinstein was one of the biggest names in Hollywood, whose films had amassed multiple Oscar awards. However, in October 2017, the *New York Times* ran an article reporting that over a dozen women had accused Weinstein of sexual harassment or assault.[11]

Soon a rapidly increasing number of women started publicly identifying themselves as victims of Weinstein's, including well-known actresses such as Gwyneth Paltrow, Cara Delevingne and Angelina Jolie.

On 15th October 2017, in response to the revelations about Weinstein, actress Alyssa Milano posted on Twitter: 'If all the women who have been sexually harassed or assaulted wrote "Me too" as a status, we might give people a sense of the magnitude of the problem.' Women did exactly that. Soon #MeToo was trending online around the world as millions of women posted that they too had been victims of sexual harassment.

Weinstein was arrested and charged with multiple accounts of sexual misconduct and sexual assault. He was stripped of his CBE, expelled from the Academy of Motion Pictures Arts and Sciences, and sentenced to twenty-three years in prison.

But this was just the beginning of the #MeToo movement. #MeToo inspired many more women, and some men, to come forward and report that they too had been victims of sexual harassment often by men in power. In October 2018, almost exactly one year on from Alyssa Milano's original tweet, the *New York Times* published a list of over 200 male leaders from the worlds of film, TV, politics, journalism and business who had lost jobs or positions following sexual harassment or sexual assault reports, since the start of the #MeToo campaign.[12] Among these were some famous names including news anchor Matt Lauer and Roman Polanski who was the Director of Motion Pictures Arts and Sciences. Also included in the list was Bill Hybels, the former lead pastor of the megachurch Willow Creek Church in Illinois, who resigned in April 2018 following multiple reports of sexual misconduct.

At the close of 2017, *Time Magazine* paid tribute to the women who drove the #MeToo movement, by awarding their famous 'Person of the Year' title to 'The Silence Breakers – The Voices that Launched a Movement.' The cover of the magazine issue featured five women: Ashley Judd (one of the first high-profile Weinstein accusers), Susan Fowler (who reported the sexual assault cases she experienced as an Uber employee), Taylor Swift (who brought radio DJ David Mueller to court over groping), Adama Iwu (who founded the lobby group We Said Enough) and Isabel Pascual (the pseudonym for a Mexican strawberry-picker who shared her story of sexual harassment). The cover also featured the arm of a sixth woman whose face was not visible, representing those who have anonymously come forward to report sexual harassment.

#MeToo has undoubtably been one of the most galvanising and inspiring social justice campaigns in modern times. Through the brave testimonies of millions globally, hundreds of sexual abusers have been brought to justice, many women have felt empowered to call out sexual harassment, and a bright public spotlight has been shone on toxic workplace cultures where powerful men abuse their positions of authority.

Watch Your Language

In the modern information age that facilitated the #MeToo campaign, another interesting aspect of modern feminism is the use of, and emphasis on, language. There are now several words and phrases that are in common parlance today but that thirty years ago would have been a foreign language. For example: 'toxic masculinity' refers to stereotypically masculine traits that propagate a patriarchal culture, such as bullying, aggression and misogyny. 'Male privilege' is the term used to refer to the system of advantages men receive merely by virtue of being male. And 'mansplaining' refers to a man patronisingly or condescendingly explaining something to a woman.

But what is perhaps even more interesting than the creation of new terminology, is the re-classification of certain common words and phrases as unacceptable and 'politically incorrect.' There are lots of examples of this.

The Marylebone Cricket Club (MCC) is based at Lord's Cricket Ground in London, and since 1788, it has been the recognised international authority on the rules of cricket. In September 2021, the MCC announced that it was changing the word 'batsman' to the gender-neutral term 'batter,' with immediate effect. Their statement explained, 'MCC believes that the use of gender-neutral terminology helps reinforce cricket's status as an inclusive game for all.'[13]

In February 2021, the toy-making company Hasbro announced that they were going to rebrand their 'Mr Potato Head' (from the Toy Story films) toys, to the new gender-neutral name 'Potato Head.' Hasbro explained: 'Hasbro is making sure all feel welcome in the Potato Head world by officially dropping the Mr from the Mr Potato Head brand name and logo to promote gender equality and inclusion.'[14]

However, possibly the boldest reclassifying of a word as unacceptable came in February 2018 during a political townhall meeting with the Canadian Prime Minister Justin Trudeau in Edmonton, Canada. Trudeau was asked a long question by a female audience member, which included the sentence: 'That's going to change the future of mankind.' Trudeau interrupted the questioner and explained to the audience and the watching media that he wanted people to stop using the word 'mankind' and instead to use the gender-neutral word 'peoplekind.'[15] The audience erupted in applause at Trudeau's gender-neutral exhortation, although very quickly, criticisms started coming in on social media, including from some who accused Trudeau of 'mansplaining.'

There are many other examples of this sort of reclassification of common vocabulary as politically incorrect. But these brief examples demonstrate the modern feminist drive to unearth and deconstruct the patriarchy wherever it may be found, including the ostensible sexism embedded in the common words and phrases people use.

What is a Woman?

From the dawning moment of First Wave Feminism, feminists have always had their critics and opponents, as well as plenty of disagreement within the movement itself.

Today the feminist movement is diverse and differences of opinion within the movement have surfaced on a variety of topics. But one issue in particular that has attracted significant attention is how feminists should engage with the trans movement. We will be dedicating the entirety of Chapter 4 to looking at the history, stories and principles of modern trans activism. However, our purpose here is to explore some of the stories of what happens when these two big social justice movements meet.

As we shall see in Chapter 4, one of the key principles at the heart of transgender activism is the right of trans individuals to self-identify and live as their gender identity rather than their 'sex assigned at birth.' Any barriers that society erects that prevents individuals doing this is called out as 'transphobic.' Therefore in the eyes of many in the trans lobby, a biological male who self-identifies as a female should have the right to be recognised and treated as a female by everyone in all circumstances. The question that feminists face is: do they agree? Or to put it another way: what is a woman?

In 2019, the Liberal Democrat Party elected its first female leader Jo Swinson. The year before, Swinson had published a book titled *Equal Power: Gender Equality and How to Achieve It*, and her Twitter bio at the time described her as a 'Remainer. Runner. Feminist.' In December 2019, Swinson appeared on BBC Radio 5 Live where she was asked by a female caller: 'Please can you tell me what a woman is?' Looking uneasy, and after considerable hesitation, Swinson answered: 'Well, I know I'm a woman. And I think we... know what we are. And I think all women are important and their rights need to be protected.' After extensive pressing from the host and caller, Swinson was still unable (or unwilling) to define a woman. Some feminists however, have not been so non-committal.

We met Germaine Greer earlier in the chapter, as one of the leading thinkers and campaigners behind Second Wave Feminism. In her 1999 book *The Whole Woman,* Greer argues that people who are biologically male should not be classed as female, even if they self-identity as female, and even if they have surgically transitioned. Greer goes on: 'Sex-change surgery is profoundly conservative in that it reinforces sharply contrasting gender roles by shaping individuals to fit them.'[16] Greer's argument is that feminists ought to be deconstructing gender stereotypes and gender roles so as to be inclusive of the whole diversity of people, rather than changing people's anatomy in order to make them fit society's gender roles, and reinforcing those gender roles in the process.

Since the publication of *The Whole Woman,* Greer had remained relatively silent on the issue of transgenderism. But in November 2015, that all changed after she was invited to give a lecture at Cardiff University on the title of 'Women and Power: The Lessons of the 20th Century.' A campaign arose amongst the university students to ban Greer from speaking. The petition website, that gathered nearly 3,000 signatures, accused Greer of 'continually misgendering trans women and denying the existence of transphobia altogether'[17] and so argued that 'hosting a speaker with such problematic and hateful views towards marginalised and vulnerable groups is dangerous.'[17] Greer fought back and managed to deliver the lecture, where she addressed her opponents directly, saying: 'Being a woman is a bit tricky. If you didn't find your pants full of blood when you were 13 there's something important about being a woman you don't know. It's not all cake and jam.'[18]

Another famous name who has chosen to dive into this controversy with both feet is *Harry Potter* author J. K. Rowling. In June 2020, Rowling retweeted an article titled 'Creating a more equal post-COVID-19 world for people who menstruate,'[19] and attached the comment: "People who menstruate." I'm sure there used to be a word for those people. Someone help me out. Wumben? Wimpund? Woomud?' Rowling received furious backlash on social media, with many labelling her as a 'TERF'- a 'Trans-Exclusionary Radical Feminist.' However, seemingly undeterred by the Twitter-storm she was generating, Rowling continued to Tweet: 'If sex isn't real, there's no same-sex attraction. If sex isn't real, the lived reality of women globally is erased. I know and love trans people, but erasing the concept of sex removes the ability of many to meaningfully discuss their lives. It isn't hate to speak the truth.'

There were several famous names that joined the chorus of condemnation of Rowling's views, including Harry Potter himself – Daniel Radcliff – who released a statement via the Trevor Project (a suicide prevention charity for LGBTQ+ youth) saying: 'I feel compelled to say something at this moment. Transgender women are women. Any statement to the contrary erases the identity and dignity of transgender people…' In December 2021, the US Quidditch and Major League Quidditch leagues, which organise real-life matches based on the fictional game in the *Harry Potter* books, announced in a joint statement that they were changing their names. This was, in part, to distance themselves from Rowling and her 'anti-trans positions.'[20] Both organisations now use the term 'quadball' rather than 'quidditch.'

Following her tweets, it was reported that employees at the Hachette publishing group, who were publishing Rowling's new children's book *The Ickabog* started refusing to work on her book. However, Hachette then released a statement announcing that staff were not permitted to refuse to work on Rowling's book because:

> Freedom of speech is the cornerstone of publishing…We will never make our employees work on a book whose content they find upsetting for personal reasons, but we

draw a distinction between that and refusing to work on a book because they disagree with an author's views outside their writing[21].

So, returning to the question posed to Jo Swinson: what is a woman? As demonstrated by the controversy surrounding Greer and Rowling, this most fundamental of questions has caused deep division amongst some feminists. People like Greer and Rowling, perhaps representing a generally older company of feminists, argue that biological sex is intrinsically linked to the unique oppression women experience, and therefore to deny the importance of biological sex is to undermine the whole purpose of feminism. This was Simone de Beauvoir's argument when she wrote back in 1949: 'Woman has ovaries, a uterus; these peculiarities imprison her in her subjectivity, [and] circumscribe her within the limits of her own nature.'[3] However, other, often younger, feminists argue that to question the femininity of a transgender female would be an act of bigoted discrimination and oppression, the kind of which feminism is meant to be fighting against.

Conclusion

It is difficult to summarise the modern feminist movement. In a sense, that is one of its defining characteristics. The feminist movement began with campaigners fighting for legal change: on voting, pay, contraception and abortion rights. However, in the last few decades, the feminist movement has rapidly evolved and expanded to cover a much bigger and more wide-reaching vision for society. According to the mainstream modern feminist narrative, society as a whole is fundamentally patriarchal – built in a way that empowers and solidifies male privilege whilst oppressing and silencing women. This patriarchy needs smashing wherever it may be found, whether it be in lecture halls, general elections, clothing, language, sports rules, fantasy books or children's toys.

2. Racial Justice

'I only knew that I was tired of being pushed around'
Rosa Parks, My Story

'We have a lot of issues in this country that we need to deal with. We have a lot of people that are oppressed.'
Colin Kaepernick, post-match interview

We now turn to the topic of race and the fight for racial justice. As mentioned in the previous chapter, we are limiting our scope in this book mostly to events in the UK and US. In light of this, and with the topic of race in particular, it is worth acknowledging that this is a tiny snapshot of the huge range of race issues and conflicts across the world today.

Like the last chapter, we begin with a condensed history of the civil rights movements, before then turning to the modern day, and the events and stories that make up today's racial justice movement.

Slavery and The Abolitionists

The origins of the Transatlantic Slave Trade can be traced as far back as the 1480s when Portuguese ships started shipping African slaves to work on sugar plantations in the eastern Atlantic islands. But by the eighteenth century, the slave trade had grown to an enormous international industry, which in total would see around twelve million Africans captured and shipped to Europe and America to carry out forced manual labour in plantations, mines, fields, construction sites and homes.[1] Many enslaved people died on the slave ships, and for those who became labourers, it is generally estimated that they had a life expectancy in the twenties.[2,3]

In April 1791, the thirty-two-year-old Yorkshire MP William Wilberforce introduced the first UK parliamentary bill to abolish the slave trade. Wilberforce passionately argued in parliament that enslaved people were fellow 'men of humanity,' and 'in my investigation of the slave trade... so enormous, so dreadful, so irremediable did its wickedness appear that my own mind was completely made up for the abolition.'[4] His 1791 bill was defeated by MPs, but it began a sixteen-year campaign to abolish the slave trade through parliament. At the core of the UK abolitionist movement were parliamentarians such as Charles Fox and Lord William Grenville, as well as a small campaigning group of evangelical Christians called the 'Clapham Sect' whose members included Wilberforce and Rector of Clapham, John Venn. After a long series of campaigns and parliamentary votes, in February 1807, parliament voted in favour of the abolition of the slave trade, with the Slave Trade Act receiving royal assent the following month. However, the practice of slavery itself remained legal in the UK until 1833 when it was finally abolished through the passing of the Slavery Abolition Act.

The road to abolitionism in the US took a very different route. When Abraham Lincoln was elected US President in March 1861, America was a house divided. Seven southern states (which eventually grew to eleven) had recently formed the breakaway 'Confederate States of America.' One of the key unifying factors amongst these Confederate States was that their economies were heavily reliant on African slave labour – something that many northern states had abolished by that time. In April 1861, the American Civil War began between the southern Confederacy states and the northern Union states – a four-year war that became the deadliest in American history. The issue of slavery quickly became central to the conflict, and in January 1863 Lincoln issued an emancipation proclamation, declaring that all slaves in all states 'shall be then, thenceforward, and forever free.' In freeing millions of slaves in Confederate States, Lincoln removed a large section of the Confederacy labour force, and many black soldiers subsequently joined the Union Army. The Civil War came to an end in 1865, and in December of that same year, the ratification of the 13th Amendment to the US Constitution formally outlawed slavery nationwide (except as a punishment for crime). Then in 1868, the adoption of the 14th Amendment granted former slaves 'equal protection' under the constitution, and in 1870, the 15th Amendment enshrined the right to vote for all citizens regardless of 'race, color or previous condition of servitude.'

Jim Crow Laws and Civil Rights Activists

Despite the abolition of slavery and the granting of constitutional equality, Africans living in America after the Civil War still faced a long uphill struggle for integration into American society. Following the end of the Civil War, southern state governments started instituting segregation laws which became known as 'Jim Crow Laws' (after the theatre character Jim Crow who was an African American depicted by a white actor wearing blackface makeup). By the 1890s, many schools in southern states were segregated by race, as well as public transport systems, theatres, hotels, restaurants and other institutions.

In 1896, state segregation laws were tested in the US Supreme Court in the landmark case 'Plessy v Ferguson.' Homer Plessy was a mixed-race man from Louisiana who was arrested for disobeying the state's Separate Car Act which segregated railroad carriages. The judge ruled that these segregation laws did not violate the 14th Amendment and therefore were constitutional. This ruling established the principle that black and white people were 'separate but equal' under US law. During this time, violent hostility against black people was increasing across America.

In February 1909, W. E. B. Du Bois and a group of fellow civil rights activists formed the National Association for the Advancement of Colored People (NAACP), which was based in New York City and whose mission was to abolish forced segregation and 'to promote equality of rights and eradicate caste or race prejudice among citizens of the United States.' By 1919, the NAACP had grown to about 90,000 members across over 300 local branches around America.

In December 1955, the secretary of the Montgomery branch of the NAACP was riding a bus in Montgomery, Alabama, when the driver instructed her to give up her seat for a white man. Her name was Rosa Parks. Montgomery's segregation ordinances stated that black passengers had to sit at the back of buses and had to give up their seats to white passengers if the front seats were filled. However, Parks refused. In her autobiography, *My Story*, Parks recalls: 'I had no idea when I refused to give up my seat... that my small action would help put an end to the segregation laws in the South. I only knew that I was tired of being pushed around.'[5] Parks was arrested and charged with disorderly conduct and violating a local ordinance. Over the following days, civil rights leaders organised a mass boycott of the Montgomery Bus Service, causing the service to lose the majority of its riders quite literally overnight. The boycott was spearheaded by a young twenty-six-year-old Baptist pastor called Martin Luther King Jr. The boycott lasted over a year and pushed the Montgomery Bus Service to near bankruptcy. Finally in November 1956, the Supreme Court declared that the Service's segregation policy was unconstitutional.[6] It was quickly repealed and the following month, King called the boycott to an end. Parks then became one of the first passengers to ride the newly de-segregated bus service.

Four years later, in February 1960, four black students in Greensboro, North Carolina, sat down for lunch at their local Woolworth's branch. However, the staff declined to serve them because of the branch's 'whites-only' policy. The students refused to leave and simply sat at their table until the place closed. The following day, they returned to the Woolworth's to do the same thing, this time joined by other students. The 'Greensboro sit-in' sparked a movement of similar 'sit-ins' around the country as hundreds of young black people peacefully went to lunch counters, sat at available spaces, and then refused to leave when service was denied because of their race. The Greensboro sit-in also prompted the formation of the Student Nonviolent Coordinating Committee (SNCC) – a movement of students who organised sit-ins, boycotts, and other non-violent protests.

In April 1963 a bus boycott also began in the UK, no doubt inspired by Rosa Parks and the Montgomery Bus Boycott. At the time, the Bristol Omnibus Company appeared to be refusing to hire black or Asian staff members. A small group of West Indian men decided to test this by arranging one of them to have a job interview with the company. The interview was granted, but when the company was then informed that the applicant was West Indian, the interview was rescinded. In response, the group organised a boycott of the company, gathering thousands of supporters including the then leader of the Labour party Harold Wilson. In August 1963, following mounting pressure, the general manager of the Bristol Omnibus Company announced that there would no longer be discrimination in their employment procedures. Two years later, the UK parliament passed the 1965

Race Relations Act, which banned racial discrimination in public places. This law was superseded by the 1976 Race Relations Act, and then again by the Equality Act in 2010.

In August 1963, on the same day that the Bristol Omnibus Company manager announced the end of discrimination in their employment procedures, Asa Philip Randolph and Baynard Rustin organised the 'March on Washington for Jobs and Freedom.' The march became one of the largest political rallies in US history. According to historian Taylor Branch, over 2000 buses, 21 trains, 10 aircraft and an uncountable number of cars converged on Washington DC, culminating in around 250,000 protesters marching from the Washington Monument to the Lincoln Memorial.[7] At the Lincoln Memorial, a series of keynote speakers addressed the crowd, including SNCC chairman John Lewis and NAACP executive secretary Roy Wilkins. But it was the final speech of the day that became one of the pivotal moments in the US civil rights movement and one of the most iconic speeches in modern history. Martin Luther King Jr. took to the podium for just sixteen minutes. He began by painting a grim picture of 'the chains of discrimination'[8] faced by black Americans, before urging his listeners to make a stand for racial justice. He then closed with what became the most famous words of his speech:

> I have a dream that one day on the red hills of Georgia, the sons of former slaves and the sons of former slave owners will be able to sit down together at the table of brotherhood... I have a dream that my four little children will one day live in a nation where they will not be judged by the color of their skin but by the content of their character. I have a *dream* today!...[8]

Finally in 1964, Congress passed the Civil Rights Act which prohibited discrimination and segregation based on 'race, color, religion, sex, or national origin.'

Into the Present

With this brief historical context in place, we now turn to the racial justice movements of the modern day. Like feminism, the campaigns for racial justice have rapidly evolved and changed over recent years. The civil rights movements of the eighteenth and early nineteenth centuries on both sides of the Atlantic focussed largely on the abolition of slavery. In the twentieth century, the focus of activists was more on outlawing segregation and direct, legally sanctioned discrimination. Some of these themes have carried on into the twenty-first century. However, many of today's racial justice movements have much broader goals, often culminating in widespread institutional and societal transformation and the deconstruction of 'white privilege.'

White Privilege

One of the most striking manifestations of this broader set of goals of the modern racial justice movement is the popularisation of the phrase 'white privilege.' The term 'white privilege' can be traced back to Theodore W. Allen's 1967 book *Can White Workers Radicals Be Radicalized?* However, the phrase was popularised in UK discourse by writers including Reni Eddo-Lodge in her best-selling book *Why I'm No Longer Talking to White People About Race*. Eddo-Lodge defines 'white privilege' as: 'the fact that if you're white, your race will almost certainly positively impact your life's trajectory in some way. And you probably won't even notice it'[9]. According to Eddo-Lodge, 'white privilege' is not a benign quirk of being white; rather it is 'a manipulative, suffocating blanket of power that envelops everything we know... It's brutal and oppressive.'[9]

A similar point is made by another best-selling book of the racial justice movement: *White Fragility* by Robin DiAngelo. DiAngelo argues that 'racism is a structure, not an event,'[10] which stems from a widespread and institutionalised 'definition of whites as the norm or standard for human, and people of color as a deviation from that norm.'[10] She then goes on to argue that white people are generally oblivious to this societal assumption and therefore complicit in the propagation of racism.

In the eyes of Eddo-Lodge and DiAngelo the current barriers to racial equality are not segregation or legally sanctioned discrimination. Rather the key problem is that society is built in a way that is fundamentally biased against ethnic minorities and is programmed to propagate structural racism. Therefore, the solution to structural racism must begin with educating white people on their privilege.

This worldview, that sees society as structurally and fundamentally biased against ethnic minorities, has formed the foundations of several areas of academic study. These include the study of 'Critical Race Theory' (which we shall be returning to in Chapter 5), and the broader 'Whiteness Studies' (or 'Critical Whiteness Studies'), both of which are now widely taught in universities across the UK and US. According to the *Oxford Research Encyclopaedia*, 'Critical Whiteness Studies' (CWS) aims to 'reveal the invisible structures that produce and reproduce white supremacy and privilege... CWS examines the meaning of white privilege and white privilege pedagogy, as well as how white privilege is connected to complicity in racism....'[11]

However, the ideas of 'white privilege' and 'whiteness studies' have triggered some backlash, particularly from those who view the generalising of all white people as complicit in racism, as itself racist. For example, political commentator Douglas Murray, commenting on the *Oxford Research Encyclopaedia's* definition of 'Critical Whiteness Studies' argues that 'defining an entire group of people [white people], their attitudes, pitfalls and moral associations, based solely on their racial characteristics is itself a fairly good demonstration of racism.'[12]

But despite such protestations, the concept of 'white privilege' is now an increasingly common part of both academic and everyday discourse, and it is beginning to manifest in real-world change.

Positive Discrimination

We discussed positive discrimination in the last chapter with reference to feminism and the drive toward greater representation of women across society. Positive discrimination is also a key issue for many campaigners for racial justice.

In *Why I'm No Longer Talking to White People About Race*, Reni Eddo-Lodge argues that positive discrimination is necessary because the structural biases and prejudices that disadvantage ethnic minorities are so deeply engrained in society that they need systematic rebalancing. She then goes on to argue that opposing positive discrimination means

> inadvertently revealing what you think talent looks like... Because, if the current system worked correctly, and if hiring practices were successfully recruiting and promoting the right people for the right jobs in all circumstances, I seriously doubt that so many leadership positions would be occupied by white middle-aged men.[9]

There are several pertinent examples of positive discrimination being deployed to increase representation of ethnic minorities.

In 2003, America's National Football League (NFL) introduced the so-called 'Rooney Rule' policy, which was named after the former chairman of the NFL's diversity committee Dan Rooney. The policy states that all NFL teams which have head coaching vacancies must interview at least one black or ethnic minority candidate, although there is no obligation to short-list or hire this person. The policy has subsequently expanded, and since 2021, teams now need to interview at least two minority candidates for head coaching positions, with some other senior NFL jobs also having similar requirements. The Rooney Rule has also now crossed the Atlantic. In 2018 the English Football Association announced that it was adopting a version of the

Rooney Rule, and in 2019, the English Football League did likewise.

But as with women-only shortlists, positive discrimination in favour of ethnic minorities has been far from uncontroversial. One area in which positive discrimination has been particularly contentious is in US university admissions. In 2013, the US Supreme Court ruled that although explicit racial quotas for university admissions are not permitted, universities are allowed to consider race in admission processes, with the intention of increasing ethnic diversity.[13] However, in 2014, a group of Asian America students filed a lawsuit against Harvard University, arguing that Harvard's 'race conscious' admission policy was unlawfully discriminating against Asian students, whose admission numbers were seemingly being kept artificially low.[14] The Massachusetts District Court ruled against the students, upholding Harvard's admission process as lawful.[14]

Unconscious Bias

Another way in which activists are trying to illuminate and deconstruct white privilege is through the advocacy for, and roll-out of, 'unconscious bias training.' Authors such as Robin DiAngelo argue that one of the reasons why white privilege and structural racism are so ubiquitous and difficult to change is because people's racial prejudices and discriminatory biases are 'largely unconscious'[10] – unknown to the implicated individual.

There are many psychological studies that can be cited to back-up the idea that humans have deep unconscious biases against certain races. For example, a review article of a range of studies, published by *Social Psychology Quarterly,* concluded: 'Research on implicit prejudice provides good evidence that most persons have deeply held negative associations with minority groups that can lead to subtle discrimination without conscious awareness.'[15]

In 1998, Harvard University released the first well-known unconscious bias test, called the 'Implicit Association Test'

(IAT), which can be done for free on their website. As the website notes, the purpose of IAT is to 'educate the public about bias' and 'it indicates that most Americans have an automatic preference for white over black [people].'[16] Since Harvard's IAT, a plethora of unconscious bias tests and unconscious bias training courses have been created and rolled-out in workplaces around the world. Organisations that have now mandated some form of unconscious bias training for their employees range from the US Department of Justice, to Google, to Starbucks.

But despite its widespread utilisation, unconscious bias training has met criticism, largely because of the lack of strong evidence for its effectiveness. For example, in 2020, the UK's Government Equalities Office commissioned a report on the evidence for unconscious bias training. The report concluded that 'there is currently no evidence that this training changes behaviour in the long term or improves workplace equality in terms of representation of women, ethnic minorities or other minority groups.'[17] Following this report, the UK government announced that it would be phasing out unconscious bias training in its departments.[18]

Despite such criticism however, unconscious bias training is now a global industry, with an estimated $8 billion per year spent on it in the US alone.[19]

Hands Up, Don't Shoot

For many campaigners, racial justice is far more than simply trying to shape culture and redress inequalities in the workplace; it is a matter of life and death.

A large 2020 study in the *Journal of Epidemiology and Community Health* found that between 2015–2020, the number of fatal police shootings of unarmed black people in the US was about three times higher than amongst white people, and these figures have remained relatively constant throughout the five-year study period.[20] The researchers described these findings as a 'public health emergency.'[20] Several of these deaths have hit international headlines.

In February 2012, seventeen-year-old Trayvon Martin was walking back from the shops in Sanford, Florida, when George Zimmerman, a volunteer for Neighbourhood Watch, saw Martin and reported him to the Sanford Police on the grounds that he looked suspicious. After a reported altercation between the two, Zimmerman shot and killed Martin. Zimmerman claimed that he shot out of self-defence, and in June 2013, Zimmerman was acquitted of murder and manslaughter. Shortly after the acquittal of Zimmerman, the hashtag #BlackLivesMatter started being used on social media, and a petition demanding the prosecution of Zimmerman reached over 2.2 million signatures.

In 2013, Patrisse Cullors, Alicia Garza and Opal Tometi formed the Black Lives Matter (BLM) Network. According to their website, BLM was founded 'in response to the acquittal of Trayvon Martin's murderer' and their mission is to 'eradicate white supremacy and build local power to intervene in violence inflicted on Black communities by the state and vigilantes.'

In August 2014, eighteen-year-old Michael Brown was caught on camera appearing to steal a box of cigars in Fergusson, Missouri. Police officer Darren Wilson received the police dispatch call and drove up to Brown. After a confrontation, Wilson fatally shot Brown. In court, Wilson claimed that he shot Brown in self-defence, and in November 2014, the grand jury reached the decision to not indict Wilson. Brown's death triggered protests around Fergusson, and Brown's stepfather was photographed holding a placard that read: 'Ferguson police just executed my unarmed son!!!' Protesters started using the slogan 'Hands Up, Don't Shoot' in solidarity with Brown – a chant that was soon adopted by other BLM protests.

In May 2020, in the midst of the COVID-19 pandemic, forty-six-year-old George Floyd was arrested in Minneapolis by four police officers on suspicion of using a counterfeit $20 bill. Floyd was handcuffed at gunpoint and placed on the ground. Then police officer Derek Chauvin knelt on Floyd's neck for 9 minutes and 29 seconds, killing Floyd. The events were captured by onlookers on phone cameras, and the videos and images quickly circulated round the world. Floyd's death triggered huge BLM protests in every state in America as well as in over sixty other countries. A *New York Times* article in July 2020 estimated that between 15 and 26 million people participated in the 2020 BLM protests, making it one of the largest movements in American history.[21]

The 2020 BLM protests in America were largely peaceful,[22] although there was significant vandalism and damage to property, which news website Axios estimated to have costed over $1 billion.[23] Part of the reason for this bill was that some demonstrators protested by tearing down statues of historical figures with links to white supremacy and slavery. Several statues of Confederate leaders such as Charles Linn and Robert E. Lee were toppled by protesters with others subsequently being removed by city authorities. Multiple statues of Christopher Columbus were also pulled down due to his links with slavery and violence against the indigenous populations of the Caribbean. In the UK, a statue of the eighteenth century MP and slave-trader Edward Colston was toppled by protesters and thrown in Bristol Harbour. Four of the protesters responsible for tearing down Colston's statue were subsequently cleared of criminal damage by Bristol Crown Court.[24]

Derek Chauvin was convicted of second-degree murder, and in June 2021 was sentenced to 22.5 years in custody.

Show Your Solidarity

As well as protests on the streets, the killings of black Americans by US police officers have also produced a movement of symbols of solidarity with black people against police brutality.

In September 2016, the San Francisco American Football Team the 49ers' walked out to face their opponents the San Diego Chargers in their final preseason game. As the US national anthem was sung, 49ers quarterback Colin Kaepernick dropped to one knee. Kaepernick explained the meaning of his kneeling in an interview after the match: 'The message is that we have a lot of issues in this country that we need to deal with. We have a lot of people that are oppressed. We have a lot of people that aren't treated equally, aren't given equal opportunities. Police brutality is a huge thing that needs to be addressed.'[25]

A few days later, the National Football League (NFL) season began, and many NFL players started following Kaepernick's lead and 'taking the knee' during the national anthem. Since then, the protest of taking the knee has grown and featured in a range of sporting contexts.

In the summer of 2021, the England men's football team made it to the UEFA Euro finals – their first major final in 55 years. Throughout the tournament, the England team took the knee before matches, with the Football Association explaining on Twitter: 'our players will... take the knee as a show of solidarity with the Black community, including members of our squad who themselves continue to suffer abuse on a regular basis.' Although the symbol was generally supported and applauded by English supporters, the team also met criticism for their kneeling. Some fans booed their national team as they took the knee, whilst UK Home Secretary Priti Patel said of the players in a TV interview: 'I just don't support people participating in that type of gesture politics.'[26]

Another notable movement of solidarity came in June 2020, following the murder of George Floyd, when music executives Brianna Agyemang and Jamila Thomas called for a day in which ordinary business activities were interrupted to reflect on and protest against racial injustice. The campaign gained popularity on social media and became known as 'Blackout Tuesday.'

On Tuesday 2nd June 2020, tens of millions of people posted a black square on Facebook and Instagram with the hashtag #BlackOutTuesday. Spotify added 8 minutes and 46 seconds of silence (the initially reported length of time Derek Chauvin compressed George Floyd's neck) to some of its playlists and podcasts. Multiple US TV channels similarly went off-air for 8 minutes and 46 seconds, and in the UK, ITV's show *This Morning* began with a statement from ITV which read: 'We stand in solidarity with our black colleagues, storytellers and viewers around the world because #BlackLivesMatter.'

As these symbols and statements of solidarity show, BLM and the racial justice movement are proving a huge force for change in society. Not only can they draw millions onto the streets in protest, but their influence is now undeniable in arenas as diverse as sport, social media, politics, music and television.

Conclusion

Today's racial justice movement finds many of its foundations in the anti-segregation campaigns of the twentieth century, nearly sixty years on from Martin Luther King's speech at the 'March on Washington for Jobs and Freedom.' However, in the past few decades the racial justice movement has grown and broadened, and for many campaigners the goals now include the total transformation of society, the deconstruction of white privilege, and the ending of institutionalised racism. Despite their critics, the impacts of these campaigns can now be seen across society: from Facebook to football, from cable TV to college courses, and from mandatory training to music streaming.

3. Gay Pride

'You have to give them hope... hope for a better place to come to if the pressures at home are too great'
Harvey Milk, San Francisco Gay Freedom Day Parade

'We imagine a world where all LGBTQ+ people are free to be themselves and we can live our lives to the full.'
Stonewall, About Us

The Crime of Being Gay

In 1952, Alan Turing, who had been famously instrumental in the cracking of the Enigma code during World War II, was arrested in his home city of Manchester. What was his crime? Homosexual activity.

At the time, homosexual acts were illegal and punishable by imprisonment in the UK, under the Criminal Law Amendment Act (1885). Homosexual activity was also illegal in all fifty states in America, and the American Psychiatric Association classified homosexuality as a psychiatric disorder.[1]

Turing pled guilty to the charges and was convicted of homosexual activity with his partner Arnold Murray.[2] The judge gave the war hero a choice between imprisonment or chemical sterilisation; he chose the latter. In 1954, Turing died by cyanide poisoning in what many concluded to be suicide.

It was in this context, of heavy criminal prosecutions for homosexual activities, that Harry Hay founded the Mattachine Society in 1950 (initially called the 'Society of Fools') – one of the first major gay rights organisations in the world. The Society began meeting in Los Angeles to discuss raising awareness of gay rights. Membership grew slowly initially. However, the Society started to gain publicity and popularity following the arrest of Dale Jennings, one of its founding members, in 1952. By the end of the 1950s the Mattachine Society had branches in Boston, New York City, Washington DC and Chicago. In the UK in 1958, the Homosexual Law Reform Society was founded to lobby the government to decriminalise homosexuality.

But it was in 1969 that the gay rights movement exploded into the international movement we know today, beginning in a single bar in Greenwich Village, New York City.

The Birth of Pride

In the 1960s, the Stonewall Inn was a large gay bar on Christopher Street in Greenwich Village, New York City, which welcomed gay people, drag queens, homeless gay teenagers and many other individuals that were shunned by other establishments. It was also reportedly the only gay bar in the city that allowed dancing.

In the early hours of 28th June 1969, New York police stormed into the Stonewall Inn – something that was not infrequent in gay bars at the time. However, rather than dispersing like normal, the 200-strong crowd decided to stand their ground against the police raid. Soon, punches, coins, bottles and rocks were being thrown, and within a few minutes, a full-blown riot had erupted. The police officers attempted to barricade themselves inside the inn, and the rioters responded by setting the place ablaze. Eventually fire services and riot police arrived and were able to extinguish the fire and disperse the crowd. Over a dozen people were arrested and several people were injured.

The next five days saw a series of further riots on Christopher Street and the surrounding neighbourhoods, with some nights drawing thousands of protesters onto the streets. Police cars were smashed, shops were looted, windows were shattered and bins were set alight. The Mattachine Society newsletter released the following month offered their explanation of the Stonewall Riots: 'It [the Stonewall Inn] catered largely to a group of people who are not welcome in, or cannot afford, other places of homosexual social gathering... The Stonewall became home to these kids. When it was raided, they fought for it.'[3]

In the months following the Stonewall Riots, several gay rights organisations were formed, including the Gay Liberation Front and the Gay Activists Alliance.

Then in 1970, on the one-year anniversary of the first Stonewall Riot, thousands of people converged on Greenwich Village to march from there to Central Park, in the 'Christopher Street Liberation Day' march. The march appeared on the front page of the *New York Times*, and simultaneous demonstrations were carried out in Los Angeles and Chicago. The Christopher Street Liberation Day march of 1970 is now widely considered to be the first gay pride march. Within a few years, annual gay pride marches were being held across America and Europe.

In 1977, Harvey Milk became one of the first openly gay men to be elected to political office in the US, as a member of the San Francisco Board of Supervisors. In June of the following year, Milk addressed the San Francisco Gay Freedom Day Parade, in which he exhorted the crowd:

> In San Francisco, three days before Gay Pride Day, a person was killed just because he was gay. And that night, I walked among the sad and the frustrated at City Hall

in San Francisco… You have to give them hope. Hope
for a better world, hope for a better tomorrow, hope for
a better place to come to if the pressures at home are
too great.[4]

Milk commissioned the artist and activist Gilbert Baker to
design a symbol of gay pride that could represent the growing
movement. Baker unveiled his creation at the 1978 pride march:
the first rainbow flag.

In 1989, following the introduction of Section 28 of the
UK Local Government Act which stated that local authorities
must not 'publish material with the intention of promoting
homosexuality,' a group of activists including actors Ian McKellen
and Pam St Clement, and journalist Matthew Parris, formed the
gay rights charity Stonewall. Stonewall would eventually become
the largest gay rights organisation in Europe. According to their
website, the organisation 'stand[s] for lesbian, gay, bi, trans, queer,
questioning and ace (LGBTQ+) people everywhere. We imagine
a world where all LGBTQ+ people are free to be themselves
and we can live our lives to the full.'[5]

The Road to Legalisation

The road to the legalisation of homosexuality in the UK was
gradual and took many years. In 1967, parliament passed the
Sexual Offences Act, which permitted homosexual activity
providing that it was done in private and both individuals were
above age twenty-one (five years higher than the age of consent
for heterosexual activity). It took three decades of campaigning,
parliamentary votes, and a court case in the European Court
of Humans Rights,[6] before the UK finally lowered the age of
consent of homosexual acts to equal that of heterosexual acts.[7]

The period following the turn of the millennium saw a rapid
series of laws passed that expanded the rights of gay citizens.
In 2002, parliament legalised the adoption of children by single
people and gay couples,[8] and the following year, it repealed

the distinction between homosexual and heterosexual activity under the law.[9] In November 2004, parliament legalised civil partnerships[10] – the first time gay relationships were recognised by UK law. The 2010 Equality Act then prohibited discrimination on the basis of sexuality, and finally, in 2013, parliament voted in favour of the legalisation of gay marriage,[11] with the first same-sex weddings in the UK taking place on 29th March 2014.

Since the legalisation of gay marriage, several major church denominations in the UK have formally announced that they will bless gay marriages. In June 2017, the Scottish Episcopal Church became the first major UK denomination to vote, by a sizeable majority of their General Synod, to alter their Canon on Marriage to include gay couples. In 2021, the Methodist Church and then the Church of Wales also voted to bless gay marriages.

Into the Present

Even though many of these landmark legal changes have occurred in fairly recent decades, the modern gay rights movement has undergone significant evolution over the last few years, not dissimilar to the changes we saw in feminism and the racial justice movement. As we have seen, for the main part of gay rights activism history, campaigns have been largely focussed on changing and repealing national laws that discriminate against gay people. There is still some emphasis on legislative change. However, for many gay rights activists and organisations, the focus of their activism is less on parliamentary debates, and more on finding and fighting personal homophobia in both the private and public spheres, and deconstructing the societal frameworks that propagate the notion that heterosexual relationships are the standard whilst homosexual relationships are abnormal.

Back to School

One area in which the fight against homophobia can be seen to be having a profound impact is in education.

In 2011, the civil liberties group the Manifesto Club obtained government figures, through a Freedom of Information Act request, that showed that in the year 2008–2009, there had been just under 30,000 'hate speech' incidents logged and reported to Local Education Authorities, involving school children making homophobic or racist remarks. Of these, around 11,000 involved primary school children, and forty were from nurseries.[12]

The political tide appears to be moving increasingly in favour of searching for homophobia in schools. In 2013, Loughborough MP Nicky Morgan was one of 161 MPs who voted against the legalisation of gay marriage. However, in 2014, shortly following her appointment as Secretary of State for Education, Morgan changed her opinion, saying in an interview that she would probably vote in favour of gay marriage if the vote was held again.[13] Then, just one year later, in an interview with BBC Radio 4, Morgan explained that she now thought that making homophobic comments could be a sign of extremism or radicalisation that teachers may be able to pick up on in the classroom.[14] In just two years, the Education Secretary moved from opposing gay marriage to describing homophobia as a potential sign of extremism, which led the *Mirror Online* to pose the question: 'Should Nicky Morgan report herself for extremism?'[15]

In 2019, the UK government published its new guidelines for teaching sex and relationship education in schools. The guidance mandates the integrating of education about LGBTQ+ relationships into the school curriculum.[16] Stonewall described the new guidance as a 'huge step forward.'[17] The aim of the curriculum is clearly to instil in school children a view of relationships that sees gay relationships, and families parented by gay couples, as normal – just part of the diverse range of families that come in all shapes and sizes. As the guidelines imply, heterosexual relationships should not be seen as normative- a view that is sometimes termed 'heteronormativity.' Rather, homosexual and heterosexual relationships ought to be seen as equally normal and morally commendable features of our diverse society.

Of course, the drive to root out personal homophobia and deconstruct heteronormativity goes far beyond the classroom. As we shall explore shortly, we can now see these campaigns playing out in areas as diverse as holiday resort advertising, bakery shopping, and the 17th May each year which is International Day Against Homophobia, Transphobia and Biphobia.

Stop Funding Hate

On Valentines Day 2018, Olympic diver Tom Daley and his husband, film director Dustin Lance Black, announced on social media that they were expecting their first child. The announcement, which came with a photograph of the two men holding the ultrasound image of their unborn child, received over 150,000 likes on Twitter.

But not everyone was equally congratulatory. The following day, journalist Richard Littlejohn published an article in the *Daily Mail* in which he wrote:

> ...despite the fact that countless single parents do a fantastic job, I still cling to the belief that children benefit most from being brought up by a man and a woman... Here we have two men drawing attention to the fact that 'they' are having a baby. But where's the mum, the possessor of the womb which features in this photograph? She appears to have been written out of the script entirely... She is merely the anonymous incubator.[18]

Unsurprisingly (I suspect even to Littlejohn), the backlash against Littlejohn's article was fierce. The LGBTQ+ news website Pink News quickly labelled Littlejohn 'homophobic'[19] and the organisation Stop Funding Hate started a campaign pressing companies to stop advertising in the *Daily Mail*. The campaign successfully persuaded the holiday resort chain Centre

Parcs and the Southbank Centre in London (the home of the London Philharmonic Orchestra) to pull their advertising in the newspaper.

However, what is perhaps more notable than *Daily Mail* columnists generating controversy, is the array of ordinary individuals, who have not set out to draw attention or generate headlines, but who nonetheless have been publicly outed as homophobic.

The Gay Cake Case

In 2014, gay rights activist Gareth Lee placed an order for a customised cake with the Ashers Bakery Company branch in Belfast. This was six years prior to the legalisation of gay marriage in Northern Ireland, and the order was for a cake iced with pictures of the Sesame Street characters Bert and Ernie, along with the slogan 'support gay marriage.' The cake was for an event to mark International Day Against Homophobia, Transphobia and Biphobia. Ashers Bakery Company is owned by Daniel and Amy McArthur, a Christian couple who, due to their religious beliefs, decided that they were unable to produce and sell a cake with such a slogan. In light of this, the McArthurs informed Lee they couldn't make the cake and refunded the cost.

Unhappy with this act of seeming discrimination against him, Lee filed a lawsuit against Ashers Bakery. The case garnered significant media attention and brought thousands of people onto the streets in rival demonstrations. In May 2015, the County Court District Judge ruled that the Ashers Bakery had unlawfully discriminated against Lee by refusing to make his customised cake, and fined the bakery £500.[20]

However, the McArthurs chose to appeal the decision, which eventually made its way to the Supreme Court.[21] In October 2016, the Supreme Court overturned the County Court decision and exonerated the McArthurs. The judges ruled that in light of their rights to conscience and religious expression, the McArthurs could not be forced to promote a belief that they profoundly disagreed with. The judges noted that the McArthurs did not refuse to make the cake because of the sexual orientation of the customer, but rather because of the slogan that was requested. In the words of the ruling: 'the objection was to the message, not the messenger.'[21]

But the story does not end there. In 2019, Lee announced that he was taking the 'gay cake case' to the European Court of Human Rights (ECHR), not to prosecute Ashers Bakery, but to scrutinise the UK's laws which, he argued, failed to protect him from sexuality-based discrimination. However, in January 2022, over seven years after the initial cake order, the ECHR issued a press release stating that the 'gay cake case' was 'inadmissible' as Lee was 'asking the [European] Court to usurp the role of the domestic courts.'[22]

Despite these rulings from the courts against Lee, what is clear from the 'gay cake case' and the surrounding protests and debate is that for many gay rights activists, failing to endorse and facilitate progressive causes, such as the legalisation of gay marriage, is tantamount to active discrimination against gay people. It's not just about what you do and say, it's also about what you *don't* do and say. This was a lesson that was also being learned at around the same time, by the MP Tim Farron.

Is it a Sin?

In 2015, the Liberal Democrat Party elected Cumbrian MP Tim Farron as its party leader. Farron is an evangelical Christian whose personal views on sexuality have been the subject of media scrutiny from the very beginning of his tenure as party leader. Shortly after becoming leader, Farron was interviewed by Cathy Newman on Channel 4 News, in which he was asked, 'Do you think, as a Christian, that homosexual sex is a sin?' Farron chose not to give a straight answer and, despite repeated questioning from Newman, stuck to explaining his belief that everyone is sinful and is it not his place to judge the sins of others. Farron's failure to declare gay sex as 'not sinful' hit national headlines, and became the repeated refrain of Farron's leadership as the UK headed into a general election.

On 18th April 2017, Prime Minister Theresa May announced that she was calling a snap general election. The following day, Farron appeared on Channel 4 News to be interviewed again by Cathy Newman and once again, Newman pressed Farron on the question 'is homosexuality a sin?.' As in 2015, Farron reiterated his belief that it was not his place to make theological pronouncements.

Journalists and politicians lined up to condemn Farron's equivocating; Labour's John McDonnell called Farron's views 'appalling' while journalist Owen Jones described Farron on Twitter as 'an absolute disgrace.'[23]

The question of 'is gay sex a sin?' then came up in most TV appearances and broadcasted interviews Farron did, taking up a significant proportion of the Liberal Democrats' media time.

As Farron recalls in his biography *A Better Ambition*, six days into the campaign, he was informed by a close friend that his refusal to answer 'no' to the question 'is gay sex a sin?' was causing such big issues within the party that there were now threats of senior resignations. Farron chose to change tack and in a following interview with Eleanor Garnier from the BBC, he announced: 'I don't believe gay sex is a sin.'

Eventually the questions around Farron's personal beliefs about homosexuality somewhat subsided, and come election night, the Liberal Democrats increased their number of MPs by four. However, despite their electoral gains, Farron resigned as party leader. In his resignation speech, he explained that his departure was a direct consequence of the questions about his faith and views on homosexuality, saying:

> The consequences of the focus on my faith is that I have found myself torn between living as a faithful Christian

and serving as a political leader…To be a political leader
– especially of a progressive, liberal party in 2017– and
to live as a committed Christian, to hold faithfully to the
Bible's teaching, has felt impossible for me.[24]

By his own admission, Farron found it impossible to lead a
liberal, progressive political party whilst holding to his personal
views on sexuality. The media and his critics made their opinions
clear; in their eyes, refusing to say gay sex is not a sin was an
irredeemable sign of personal homophobia.

Why Did the Chicken Cross the Pond?

Chick-fil-A is one of the biggest fast-food chains in the US,
with over 2400 restaurants across forty-seven States. One of the
company's trademarked slogans boldly claims: 'We Didn't Invent
the Chicken, Just the Chicken Sandwich.' In 2019, Chick-fil-A
attempted to crack the UK market, opening two stores: one in
Aviemore in the Scottish Highlands and one in Reading.

However, shortly after these first outlets opened in the UK, a
campaign was started urging people to boycott Chick-fil-A stores
and petition for their closure. Why? As the 'Cluck Off- No Chick
Fil A in Scotland' petition website explained: 'Chick Fil A has
for years funded several anti-LGBT organisations and causes.
Giving millions to organisations that have opposed marriage
and other rights for LGBT people.'[25] The petition website then
linked to a *Vox* article which identified the main organisations
in question who were receiving donations from Chick-fil-A.[26]
These were: the Salvation Army and the Fellowship of Christian
Athletes. It is worth noting that the focus of the campaign was
not any homophobic comments Chick-fil-A had made, nor any
reported discrimination against gay customers or employees.
Rather the issue was the views of the organisations to which
Chick-fil-A chose to donate money.

Following this pressure from activists, Chick-fil-A cut its
financial giving to the Salvation Army and the Fellowship of

Christian Athletes. The Salvation Army responded, saying in a statement that they were sad about this withdrawal of funding and: 'We serve more than 23 million individuals a year, including those in the LGBTQ+ community... In fact, we believe we are the largest provider of poverty relief to the LGBTQ+ population.'[27]

Within a year of coming to the UK, Chick-fil-A had closed both of its UK outlets.

For Chick-fil-A the issue that got them branded as an enemy of the gay rights movement was not their words or actions per se; nor was it their omissions or refusals to endorse gay rights policies. Rather, their problem, according to the activists that successfully closed them down in the UK, was their *associations*. In funding organisations that were deemed to be homophobic, Chick-fil-A was judged to be implicated in their homophobia, and therefore deserving of being boycotted and driven out of business in the UK.

A House Divided

The abbreviation LGBTQ+ (standing for lesbian, gay, bisexual, transgender, queer/questioning and others) is widely used across campaigns and organisations, and is now nearly synonymous with the gay rights movement. The different groups represented by the different letters have significant things in common – not least the discrimination they have faced and continue to face due to their sexuality or gender. However, in recent years one of the most intriguing aspects of the gay rights movement has been the conflict that has arisen from within the movement itself, specifically around the place of the T in the LGBTQ+ alliance.

In 2015, following a consultation with trans activists, Stonewall published its 'Trans People and Stonewall' report. In it, Stonewall announced its plan to become 'trans-inclusive' and openly apologised for not including trans issues in their remit up until then. Stonewall has since supported several campaigns by trans activists, including reforming the Gender Recognition Act (2004) to allow trans people to change their legally recognised gender without the need for a medical diagnosis of gender dysphoria (more on the Gender Recognition Act in the next chapter).[28]

However, not all Stonewall members have embraced this move to trans-inclusivity. For example, in 2021, Matthew Parris, who was one of Stonewall's founding members, wrote in *The Times* that 'Stonewall should stay out of [the] trans rights war' and the organisation had been 'cornered into an extremist stance.'[29]

In September 2019, twenty-two Stonewall members signed an open letter in *The Sunday Times* in which they said that Stonewall's stance on trans issues 'undermined women's sex-based rights and protections' and 'if Stonewall remains intransigent, there must surely now be an opening for a new organisation committed both to freedom of speech and to fact instead of fantasy.'[30] They kept good to their word; within weeks, a group had split from Stonewall to form the LGB Alliance. Speaking to *The Telegraph*, co-founder of the LGB Alliance Kate Harris explained:

> The main difference is that lesbians, gays and bisexuals have something in common because of our sexual orientation, that has nothing to do with being trans. We welcome the support of anyone–gay, straight or trans– as long as they support our commitment to freedom of speech and biological definitions of sex... We will be called transphobic, but we're not.[31]

As Harris predicted, several people have since labelled the LGB Alliance as 'transphobic' for their failure to support trans campaigns. This includes the Labour Campaign for Trans Rights – a group within the UK Labour Party whose '12 Pledges for Labour Party Members' specifically names the LGB Alliance as a 'transphobic organisation.'[32] In return Kate Harris branded Stonewall as 'homophobic,' arguing that if Stonewall's trans-inclusive policies were popularised, 'a lot of us lesbians, who were tomboys as children, would be encouraged to transition now.'[33] In Harris' eyes, encouraging children to explore their gender identity does not enhance liberty, but rather reinforces gender stereotypes, as feminine boys or masculine girls are urged to either conform to stereotypes, or consider transitioning. I doubt Harris could have predicted, when she was a volunteer campaigner for Stonewall, that one day she would publicly label Stonewall as 'homophobic'!

As the conflict between Stonewall and the LGB Alliance demonstrates, the issues of gay and trans rights, and how they interact, are complex and have caused heated division within the LGBTQ+ movement.

Conclusion

Ever since the Stonewall riots of 1969, the gay rights movement has transformed the lives of countless gay people and has been instrumental in the changing of a range of laws that have brought increasing legal equality between gay and straight citizens.

However, today's gay rights movement has broader goals than just legal reform. For many gay rights activists, the aim of the movement is now the deconstruction of the structures and biases that propagate heteronormativity and validate homophobia, whether they be amongst our political leaders, poultry restaurants, patisseries, or primary schools.

4. Trans Rights

'Who decided what the 'norm' should be? Why are some people punished for their self-expression?'
Leslie Feinberg, Transgender Liberation

'I'm so happy after such a long struggle to be living my true self. Welcome to the world Caitlyn.'
Caitlyn Jenner, on Twitter

The National Center for Transgender Equality in the US defines 'transgender' as 'people whose gender identity is different from the gender they were thought to be at birth.'[1] (This is different from 'intersex' which is the term used to describe the various conditions where a person's anatomy is not easily classified as biologically male or female.) According to the UK government's 2018 'Trans People in the UK' report, there are approximately 200,000- 500,000 trans people living in the UK.[2]

The transgender movement is certainly one of the youngest of the social justice movements. The reality of transgender, gender dysphoric and gender-nonconforming individuals has been arguably known about for centuries. However, it is only in the last few decades that a recognisable trans movement began to emerge.

The Fight for Recognition

In 1930, the Danish painter and fashion illustrator Lili Elbe travelled to Germany to become one of the first well-known people in the world to undergo male-to-female transition surgery. Under the scalpels of Dr Erwin Gohrbandt and Dr Kurt Warnekros, Elbe had five surgeries in total including a uterus transplant. Elbe's transition gained considerable attention from German and Danish newspapers. However, sadly in 1931, Elbe died due to post-operative complications shortly after her fifth surgery.

American singer and actress Christine Jorgensen became the first well-known individual in the US to undergo transition surgery in 1951, which catapulted her to somewhat unwanted national fame. In her autobiography, Jorgensen explains:

> Can you realize what success for me will mean to literally thousands of people?... It may mean new hope and life to so many people. I think we (the doctors and I) are fighting this the right way – make the body fit the soul, rather than vice versa. For me, it is the heart, the look in the eyes, tone of voice, and the way one thinks that makes the real person.[3]

The following year, activist and pharmacologist Virginia Prince launched the newsletter: *Transvestia: The Journal of the American Society for Equality in Dress*. Although it only ran for two issues, many regard this as the beginning of the trans rights movement. In 1960, Prince relaunched *Transvestia* as a bi-monthly magazine, mainly consisting of autobiographical stories, letters and other submissions from readers. As the inside cover of the magazine explained: 'Transvestia is dedicated to the needs of those heterosexual persons who have become aware of their "other side" and seek to express it.[4] The magazine quickly grew in popularity, reaching over a thousand subscribers by the mid-1960s. It was through the later editions of *Transvestia* that Prince is reputed to have popularised the term 'transgender' in public discourse.

Also in the 1960s, Professor of Medical Psychology John Money established the term 'gender identity' and was one of the first prominent academics to propose that someone's gender identity is not necessarily connected to their biological sex. In 1965, Money co-founded the Johns Hopkins Gender Identity Clinic, which started carrying out sex reassignment surgeries (sometimes called 'gender affirming' surgeries) the following year.

In the UK, in 1970, the early trans rights movement hit a major setback following a High Court divorce lawsuit. The case pertained to the transgender woman April Ashley who had surgically transitioned from male to female prior to her marriage to Arthur Corbett. In a landmark decision, the judge ruled that individuals cannot legally change their sex, and therefore the Corbetts' marriage was void as it was between two biological males.[5] (This was clearly well before the legalisation of gay marriage.)

In 1992, author and activist Leslie Feinberg published a pamphlet titled *Transgender Liberation: A Movement Whose Time Has Come*. Contained within the text are many themes and ideas that would set the trajectory of the modern trans movement. Feinberg writes:

> All our lives we've been taught that sex and gender are synonymous – men are "masculine" and women are "feminine"... It's just "natural," we've been told. But... simplistic and rigid gender codes are neither eternal nor natural. They are changing social concepts... Who decided what the "norm" should be? Why are some people punished for their self-expression?[6]

The pamphlet concludes with a call to revolution:

> The institutionalized bigotry and oppression we face today have not always existed. They arose with the division of society into exploiter and exploited... We are the class that does the work of the world, and can revolutionize it. We can win true liberation.[6]

Many of Feinberg's ideas have now become central themes of the modern trans movement, from the doctrine that gender is a social construct, to the centrality of self-expression, to the accusation of bigotry, to the framing of society in terms of 'oppressors versus oppressed' (or 'exploiter versus exploited' in Feinberg's words).

Transitioning Society

In the 1970s, things began to change for the trans movement. Renée Richards is an American ophthalmologist and retired professional tennis player, who surgically transitioned from male to female in 1975. However, the following year, Richards' transgender identity was publicly outed by TV presenter Richard Carlson. In response, the US Tennis Association (USTA) and several other major tennis bodies mandated that all female competitors needed to take chromosomal tests to confirm that they were biologically female. Richards refused and sued the USTA. The Supreme Court ruled in favour of Richards and barred the USTA from excluding Richards from the women's tournament. The judge branded the USTA's policy as 'grossly unfair, discriminatory and inequitable, and violative of her [Richard's] rights under the Human Rights Law of this state.'[7] This landmark ruling is generally seen as the first time that a trans person's gender identity was recognised under US law.

In 1992, Press for Change was founded, which would become one of the most influential trans rights lobby groups in the UK. One of their biggest campaigns centred on the European

Court of the Human Rights (ECHR) case 'Goodwin v United Kingdom' – a case which would lead to a major shift in UK law.

Christine Goodwin was a transgender woman who underwent surgical transitioning under the NHS in 1990. Following this, Goodwin reported experiencing sexual harassment at her place of work. After moving to a new employer, Goodwin was asked by her workplace to provide her National Insurance (NI) number. However, this made her concerned that her NI number would allow her new employer to trace information about her gender identity and transition. Furthermore, Goodwin was refused her state pension payment at age sixty, which was the retirement age for women, because her government records still listed her as male (with a retirement age of sixty-five). The ECHR ruled that the lack of recognition of transgender people's gender identity in UK law was in violation of Articles 8 and 12 of the European Convention on Human Rights – the right to private and family life, and the right to marry.[8]

Following this ruling from the ECHR, the UK parliament introduced the Gender Recognition Act in 2004. The Act enables transgender people to apply for a Gender Recognition Certificate (GRC) which facilitates legal recognition of their gender identity. For people born in the UK, the GRC also entitles individuals to a birth certificate with their recognised legal gender on it. However, to receive a GRC, there are several criteria that must be met. Most applicants have to:

- Be over 18 years old
- Have a diagnosis of gender dysphoria
- Have lived in their 'acquired gender' (this is the language used in the Act) for two years
- Intend to live permanently in their acquired gender until death

In 2018, the Government Equalities Office reported that since the introduction of the Gender Recognition Act in 2004, 4910 trans people had been issued GRCs.[2]

Into the Present

As we have already seen in this chapter, many of the key legal and societal advances of trans activism have occurred in relatively recent years. In fact, it was only in 2019 that the World Health Organisation announced it was no longer classifying transgenderism as a psychiatric disorder.[9]

However, in the last few years, the trans movement has become an international force for change, whose goals are now broader than simple legal reform, although this is still a key part of trans activism. The trans movement is now focussed on much wider societal transformation, and one of its key breakthrough moments came in 2015 on a Friday night TV interview on ABC News.

Call Me Caitlyn

In the 1970s the then-called Bruce Jenner was an American sporting hero, most famed for winning the 1976 Montreal Olympic gold medal for the decathlon with a world-record final score. Jenner was given the lofty title of 'world's greatest athlete' by many commentators, and became a household name whose publicity ranged from the cover of *Sports Illustrated* magazine to the Wheaties cereal box.

In April 2015, Jenner sat down for a two-hour interview with Diane Sawyer for ABC's news show *20/20*. However, the main topic of conversation was not sport. Fighting back tears, Jenner began the interview by explaining to Sawyer: 'I've always been very confused with my gender identity since I was this big... I look at it this way: Bruce – always telling a lie.'[10] Sawyer then directly asked Jenner: 'Are you a woman?,' to which Jenner answered: 'Um, yes. For all intents and purposes, I am a woman... I was not genetically born that way. And as of now, have all the male parts... But we still identify as female.'[10]

Around seventeen million people tuned in to watch the interview- the show's highest viewing figures in fifteen years.

In June 2015, Jenner began publicly using the pronoun 'she/her,' and the following month, she announced that she was adopting the name 'Caitlyn.' On Twitter, Jenner posted: 'I'm so happy after such a long struggle to be living my true self. Welcome to the world Caitlyn. Can't wait for you to get to know her/me.'

Caitlyn Jenner brought trans rights and trans visibility into the international spotlight. That year she appeared on the cover of *Vanity Fair* magazine with the headline 'Call Me Caitlyn,' won *Glamour* magazine's 'woman of the year' title, and received the Arthur Ashe Courage Award at the Excellence in Sports Performance Yearly awards. She also broke the record for the fastest person to reach one million followers on Twitter, hitting the milestone in just over four hours.

The world's greatest athlete had now become the world's most famous trans person.

Watch Your Language

One area where the trans movement has undoubtedly begun to shape and change society is in the use of biological language.

We saw in Chapter 1 that the controversy surrounding J. K. Rowling's views on transgenderism began following the publication of an article titled: 'Creating a more equal post-COVID-19 world for people who menstruate' by the online news website Devex[11]. The article explored how the COVID-19 pandemic has highlighted injustices affecting the 'estimated 1.8 billion girls, women, and gender non-binary persons [who] menstruate'[11]. The wording of the article was clearly chosen to be inclusive of transgender men (who self-identify as male but who have uteruses and menstrual periods) and non-binary individuals (who do not self-identify as either male or female).

This move towards gender-neutral vocabulary is not limited to online news websites.

In February 2021, Brighton and Sussex University Hospitals NHS Trust became the first NHS Trust to introduce a 'gender inclusive language policy.'[12] Its new guidelines suggest to midwives and obstetricians that they should consider using the word 'chestfeeding' rather than 'breastfeeding,' and 'parental' instead of 'maternal.' The Trust explained on Twitter that their 'approach has been carefully considered to be inclusive of trans and non-binary birthing people without excluding the language of women or motherhood.'

Brighton and Sussex NHS Trust are not the only medical institution to have adopted gender-neutral language.

In September 2021, *The Lancet,* which is one of the highest-powered medical journals in the world, published an edition with a quote on the cover that read: 'Historically, the anatomy and physiology of bodies with vaginas have been neglected.'[13] The quote was from an article within the edition titled 'Periods on Display' which explored the historical 'silence, shame, and stigma surrounding menstruation.'[13] As with the previous examples, this gender-neutral language of 'bodies with vaginas' was clearly chosen to be inclusive of trans men and non-binary individuals. However, this trans-inclusive language was not welcomed by all, with some critics branding the journal cover as sexist and degrading to women. Prof. David Curtis, who is Honorary Professor of Genetics at University College London, described the headline on Twitter as 'absolutely inexcusable language to refer to women and girls,' whilst the campaign group Women Make Glasgow described it (also on Twitter) as 'dehumanising and straight up sexist.' Following the backlash, the editor of *The Lancet* Richard Horton issued a statement apologising for the headline, saying:

> I apologise to our readers who were offended by the cover quote and the use of those same words in the review. At the same time, I want to emphasise that transgender health is an important dimension of modern

health care… Trans people regularly face stigma, discrimination, exclusion, and poor health…[14]

I recently encountered another way in which the trans movement is shaping language in healthcare when I had my COVID booster vaccine in Winter 2021. I attended a vaccination centre in my local hospital, and the nurse began by running through a list of standard questions including my personal details and drug allergies. Then, without pausing, the nurse asked me: 'is there any chance you could be pregnant?' I must have looked surprised (even under my facemask) at being asked something I had never been asked before, as she quickly followed up: 'sorry, we have to ask everyone now.'

As Brighton and Sussex NHS Trust, *The Lancet*, and my local vaccination centre show, the use of gender-neutral vocabulary, chosen to be inclusive of transgender and non-binary individuals, is becoming increasingly widespread, and is now being used by important medical institutions. However, it has not been welcomed by everyone, and in some cases has been condemned as sexist and degrading, including by some feminist activists.

Back to School

Another place where trans activism is significantly shaping policies and lives is amongst school children.

According to the figures from the Gender Identity Service, in the financial year 2010–2011, 138 children under eighteen were referred to their gender clinics. This figure then increased year on year, to 2748 children in 2019–2020[15]: a nearly twenty-fold increase in nine years.

This increase in the number of children self-identifying as transgender is now being noticed in schools. In 2018, a secondary school in Brighton published, in its Equality and Information Report, that it had forty pupils who 'do not identify as [the] gender presented at birth' and a further thirty-six who were gender-fluid (not having a fixed gender identity).[16]

In August 2021, the Scottish Government released its Supporting Transgender Pupils in Schools guidance. The wide-reaching, seventy-page document makes several notable recommendations to schools including: not dictating which toilet or changing room a transgender child should use, using the pronouns requested by the child (and apologising if the wrong pronoun is used accidentally), and making dancing events less gender-specific (including Ceilidh dancing).[17] Furthermore, teachers are advised that 'if a young person comes out to you, it's also important not to deny their identity, or overly question their understanding of their gender identity.'[17]

In Stockholm, Sweden, Egalia Pre-School has caught the world's attention for its even more comprehensive gender-neutral pedagogy[18]. In Egalia, the terms 'boy' and 'girl' are avoided, and conscious efforts are made to refer to children by their name or with the genderless pronoun 'hen' (borrowed from Finnish), in order to help raise the children free from gender expectations.

The underlying principle behind Scotland's Supporting Transgender Pupils in Schools guidance, and the approach of Egalia, is that a child's gender should not be dictated by midwives, parents or teachers, but rather by the individual's sense of self. Therefore, there is an increasingly noticeable drive to ensure children are raised and educated in a way that does not impose a gender, but rather encourages children to explore their gender identity for themselves.

However, these moves to encourage children to explore their gender identity have not been welcomed by everyone.

The De-Transitioners

We have already seen in previous chapters that there are several groups of people who have voiced opposition to some of the trans activists' policies, including some prominent feminist and gay rights campaigners. Another notable group who is worth discussing, who have also expressed concerns about some trans campaigns, is the so-call 'de-transitioners.' De-transitioners are individuals who have transitioned from one gender to another, but have then realised that the decision was wrong for them, and so have begun to transition back. Some of these people have chosen to publicly share their stories.

Walt Heyer is an American author and speaker who, at time of writing, is now in his eighties. In an article for the journal *Public Discourse*, Heyer recalled that his life was 'a life filled with gender dysphoria, sexual abuse, alcohol and drug abuse,'[19] which all began in childhood. Eventually, Heyer sought advice from a gender psychologist, and as he recalls: 'he [the gender psychologist] quickly assured me that I obviously suffered from gender dysphoria. A gender change, he told me, was the cure. Feeling that I had nothing to lose and thrilled that I could finally attain my lifelong dream, I underwent a surgical change at the age of forty-two.'[19]

However, after a period of relative contentment, Heyer started to experience deep psychological conflict which grew into depression and then suicidality. Heyer sought medical help and was eventually diagnosed with dissociative disorder. Heyer reflects:

> It was maddening. Now it was apparent that I had developed a dissociative disorder in childhood to escape the trauma of the repeated cross-dressing by my grandmother and the sexual abuse by my uncle. That should have been diagnosed and treated with psychotherapy. Instead, the gender specialist never considered my difficult childhood or even my alcoholism and saw only transgender identity. It was a quick jump to prescribe hormones and irreversible surgery.[19]

Another de-transitioner who has become a prominent campaigner against the use of puberty blockers in children is Keira Bell. When she was fifteen, Bell was referred to the Tavistock and Portman Gender Identity Clinic in London and diagnosed with gender dysphoria. As Bell recalls in a blog, she started transitioning from female to male as a teenager: 'After a series of superficial conversations with social workers, I was put on puberty blockers at age 16. A year later, I was receiving testosterone shots. When 20, I had a double mastectomy.'[20]

However, following her double mastectomy, Bell began to regret transitioning. As Bell goes on in her blog:

> But the further my transition went, the more I realized that I wasn't a man, and never would be. We are told these days that when someone presents with gender dysphoria, this reflects a person's 'real' or 'true' self, that the desire to change genders is set. But this was not the case for me. As I matured, I recognized that gender dysphoria was a symptom of my overall misery, not its cause.[20]

Five years on from when she started to medically transition, Bell began transitioning back to being female.

In March 2020, Bell filed a lawsuit against the Tavistock Clinic, arguing that children under sixteen are too young to be able to consent to medical interventions as life-changing as puberty blockers.[21] The High Court judge agreed and ruled that children are unlikely to be capable of consenting to puberty blockers, as they probably cannot understand the long-term risks and consequences. This ruling essentially prohibited all administration of puberty blockers in the UK.

However, in September 2021, following campaigns from multiple LGBTQ+ charities, the Court of Appeal overturned the High Court judgment, and ruled that it would be up to clinicians to assess whether individual children are capable of consenting to puberty blockers.[22] The transgender children's charity Mermaids welcomed the Court of Appeal decision, saying: 'This is a victory for common sense and young people's bodily autonomy.'[23]

But the story does not end there. In 2020, NHS England commissioned an independent review into the Tavistock Clinic, led by paediatrician Dr Hilary Cass. An interim report published in February 2022 criticised several aspects of the care given in the Tavistock Clinic, including the 'lack of consensus and open discussion about the nature of gender dysphoria and therefore about the appropriate clinical response' and the fact that 'the clinical approach and overall service design [of the clinic] has not been subjected to some of the normal quality controls that are typically applied when new or innovative treatments are introduced.' Cass was also critical of the lack of routine data collection by the clinic, meaning 'it is not possible to accurately track the outcomes and pathways that children and young people take through the service.'[24]

Following these criticisms, in July 2022, the NHS announced that it was shutting down the Tavistock Clinic. Keira Bell welcomed the announcement of the closure, telling BBC Radio 4's World at One programme: 'Many children will be saved from going down the path that I went down.'

Beyond the Binary

One final area worth exploring within the trans movement is the topic of non-binary gender. In recent years, there has been increasing focus amongst some trans activists on challenging the whole concept of binary gender.

The term 'genderqueer' was popularised in the 1990s by activists including Riki Anne Wilchins who used the term to refer to individuals who do not identify as either male or female.[25] The term 'gender non-binary' has since become the more commonly used term.

In 2012, the Nonbinary and Intersex Recognition Project (originally called the Intersex and Genderqueer Recognition Project) was founded, which was the first well-known organisation in the US that specifically campaigned for the recognition of gender non-binary people. According to their website, the project's aim is: 'to shift our culture and political system to recognize and celebrate nonbinary and intersex people across the US. We focus on policy efforts for third gender options (X) on state IDs and birth certificates, and support banning unnecessary medical procedures on intersex youth.'[26]

In October 2021, following campaigns and a lawsuit, Dana Zzyym became the first American to be issued with a gender-neutral passport with an 'X' in the gender box. Several other countries now also issue official personal documents with non-binary gender options including Canada, Germany and Australia.

However, there is a wide range of views amongst trans activists on how many genders actually exist.

The Royal College of General Practitioners' 2019 statement on trans healthcare mentions six recognised genders: male, female, gender neutral, non-binary, gender fluid and gender queer.[27] Stonewall's website recognises at least seventeen genders including 'agender,' 'bi-gender' and 'neutrois.'[28] And in 2014, Facebook added fifty-six new gender options (which has since increased) and users can choose more than one.

In 2019, the BBC published an educational video titled 'Identity: Understanding Sexual and Gender Identities' as part of their online Relationships and Sex Education package aimed at nine to twelve year olds. The video featured a teacher explaining to some children that 'there are over 100 if not more gender identities now.'[29] The video gained increased attention in 2020, particularly during the COVID-19 national lockdowns when online teaching materials became more widely utilised by teachers and parents. It started attracting complaints and criticisms, including from transgender actress Nicole Gibson who criticised the video in an interview with Good Morning Britain. Gibson went on to explain her opinion that 'there are two genders: male and female. Sometimes you're not lucky enough to be born into the right one so you transition into the one that you suit the most.'[30] Following the complaints, the BBC withdrew the video and responded on their website: 'We are aware that this particular film is being wilfully misinterpreted by parts of the media and others on social media. As such, its original purpose and intention has been overshadowed. On this basis we have made the decision to retire the film.'[31]

The deconstruction of binary gender is becoming an increasingly mainstream goal for trans activism. In many ways, these campaigns have been ostensibly successful and have led to countries beginning to issue non-binary passports, and large influential institutions such as Facebook and the BBC now recognising dozens, if not hundreds, of genders. However, this deconstruction of binary gender has been far from uncontroversial, with even some transgender individuals pushing back and arguing that there are only two genders that can be transitioned between.

Conclusion

Despite its relative youth compared with the other social justice movements, the trans movement has seen some major societal and legal advances in the last few years. Transition therapies are now accessible for free in the NHS, and through the campaigns of trans rights organisations and some prominent individuals, trans people are now generally seen as an integral and celebrated part of our diverse society.

However, the trans movement has also attracted criticism, including from some transgender individuals themselves. Some have challenged the safety of reassignment therapies, especially when given to children, and others have questioned if the use of gender-neutral language is sometimes demeaning to women. In addition, there is now debate amongst some trans activists around whether gender is binary, or encompasses a whole range of potentially hundreds of gender identities. But one thing is for certain; the trans movement is beginning to rapidly transform many aspects of modern society, ranging from the medical, to the legal, to the educational, to the social, to the profoundly personal.

5. The Grand Narrative of Identity Politics

'Man is born free, but everywhere he is in chains'
Jean-Jacques Rousseau, The Social Contract

'Search me, God, and know my heart'
King David, Psalm 139:23a

In the last four chapters, we set out to explore some of the key stories, events and people that have shaped our modern identity politics culture, and have driven the social justice movements of feminism, racial justice, gay pride and the trans rights movement. We have seen that each movement has its own unique history and has faced its own unique set of challenges. In addition, we have also touched on some of the occasions in which diversity of views has led to conflict, both within the individual social justice movements, and between activists from the different movements.

However, in this chapter we will begin to explore some of the key common threads that bind all of these movements together.

Despite their diversity, and sometimes their disagreements, I would suggest that the social justice movements are also fundamentally united by a bigger, over-arching story.

The Story of Identity Politics

As we follow the narratives of the identity politics movements, we can begin to see a grand metanarrative emerging.

The metanarrative of identity politics tells the story of historically oppressed identity groups, namely (but not exclusively) women, ethnic minorities, gay people and trans people, who have suffered for centuries under oppressive and discriminatory systems and institutions built by the oppressive classes. Women have been oppressed for centuries by the patriarchy; black and ethnic minorities by white supremacy and institutionalised racism; gay people by a culture of heteronormativity and deep-seated homophobia; and trans people by the systems of binary gender and transphobia.

But these oppressed groups are beginning to wake up to their oppression and in doing so, have become 'woke'- a term first publicly used in 1938 by Black American folk singer Lead Belly to refer to the need for black people to be alert to the dangers they face simply for being black in America. These oppressed individuals have then responded to their awareness of oppression by coalescing around their identity groups to form organisations and movements that are now rising up to fight against and overthrow their oppressors.

Identity politics is ultimately the story of the oppressed rising up to fight and overthrow their societal oppressors.

The History of the Identity Politics Ideas

Author Terry Pratchett once wrote: 'If you do not know where you come from, then you don't know where you are, and if you don't know where you are, then you don't know where you're going. And if you don't know where you're going, you're probably going wrong.'[1] Before we look at the modern implications of this grand narrative of identity politics, it is valuable to first look backwards to the philosophies and ideologies that paved the way for our contemporary cultural story. The history of ideas that formed identity politics is a vast topic in and of itself. Therefore what follows is just a brief summary of some of the key philosophies that have built our modern culture.

1. Philip Rieff, Robert Bellah and 'Psychological Man'

In his 1966 book *Triumph of the Therapeutic*, sociologist Philip Rieff proposes a schema of history that sees the development of human culture as divided into four eras. Rieff suggests that the first era was that of what he terms 'Political Man,' who was defined by the ideas of Plato and Aristotle. 'Political Man' was someone who was immersed in their community and whose identity was defined primarily by their political activities. However, in the Middle Ages, 'Political Man' was replaced by what Rieff calls 'Religious Man.' Much of the Medieval Period was marked by church authority and religious activities, and so 'Religious Man' was someone who was chiefly characterised not by family or politics but by religious affiliations, activities and beliefs. 'Religious Man' was subsequently succeeded by a third era: that of 'Economic Man.' As trade, finance and economic activity began to dictate lifestyles and livelihoods, and as the Industrial Revolution swept across Europe and America, 'Economic Man's' identity became tied to profession and income. However, the era of 'Economic Man' has, according to Rieff, been replaced by the fourth and current era: that of 'Psychological Man.' 'Psychological Man' sees their identity not in terms of their relation to external people, institutions or systems, but by their inner psychological convictions and their personal quest for happiness and contentment. 'Psychological Man' subscribes to the ideology that sociologist Robert Bellah terms 'expressive individualism' – the idea that meaning to life can be found through the external expression of internal emotions and desires.[2]

Rieff's summary of Western cultural anthropology gives a helpful introduction to the era that gave rise to identity politics. Identity politics has arisen from a time in history when people's sense of identity comes from aspects of their lives that are: individual rather than corporate, emotional rather than professional, and secular rather than religious.

Rieff therefore gives us some of the essential foundations of the 'identity' in 'identity politics.'

2. Jean-Jacques Rousseau and Romanticism

However, identity politics does not just see the expressive individual as supreme; it also sees the societal structures in which the individual lives as the sources of oppression and corruption. One of the key figures to whom this belief can be traced is the eighteenth century Romantic philosopher Jean-Jacques Rousseau. Rousseau proposes that humans are born with innate and natural moral virtue and innocence – in a sense, the opposite of Augustine of Hippo's doctrine of Original Sin (more on this in Chapter 10). According to Rousseau, this innate innocence is then corrupted by societal pressures and external influences[3,4] – a view he summarises in his famous adage: 'Man is born free, but everywhere he is in chains.'[5] Philosopher Charles Taylor summarises Rousseau's views as: 'The original impulse of nature is right, but the effect of a depraved culture is that we lose contact with it.'[6]

As historian Carl Trueman then points out, this view leads to the conclusion that 'if the state of nature is the ideal, and if society corrupts, then the history of society becomes the history of the corruption and oppression of human nature.'[7]

Rousseau's principles can be seen in various areas of identity politics, from the focus of 'Whiteness Studies' on the societal structures and biases that oppress ethnic minorities, to Scottish schools being told not to question the gender expression of pupils.[8] These sorts of ideas and polices have deep roots in Rousseau's belief that humans are innately innocent and that society is to blame for the oppression and corruption of their identities.

3. Karl Marx and Critical Theory

In February 1848, German philosophers Karl Marx and Friedrich Engels published *The Communist Manifesto*, which became one of the most influential political documents in history. In *The Communist Manifesto*, Marx and Engels frame society as ultimately a struggle between two economic classes: the 'Bourgeoisie' and the 'Proletariat.' The Bourgeoisie are the upper economic class who control the means of industrial production and who are chiefly concerned with the preservation of their own economic supremacy. The Proletariat are the working class who labour under oppression to produce the capital accumulated by the Bourgeoisie. *The Communist Manifesto* is a call to revolution. Marx and Engels urge the Proletariat to rise up and gain power in order to overthrow their Bourgeoisie oppressors. Here are the opening lines of Chapter 1 of *The Communist Manifesto*:

> The history of all hitherto existing societies is the history of class struggles. Freeman and slave, patrician and plebeian, lord and serf, guild-master and journeyman, in a word, oppressor and oppressed, stood in constant opposition to one another, carried on an uninterrupted, now hidden, now open fight, a fight that each time ended, either in a revolutionary re-constitution of society at large, or in the common ruin of the contending classes.[9]

In the 1930s, researchers at the Institute for Social Research in Frankfurt, which became known as the 'Frankfurt School,' built on the ideas of Marx to found the political philosophy known as 'Critical Theory.' Critical Theory took the Marxist principle of society being ultimately a power struggle between classes and expanded it beyond economic classes to encompass the broader hidden institutionalised power structures in wider society. For example, Critical Theorists may frame society not just as a power struggle between rich and poor, but between educated and uneducated, or between males and females, or between ethnic majorities and ethnic minorities. As we saw in Chapter 3, this last framing, that sees society as a power struggle between the white majority and the ethnic minorities, has become a well-established and popular academic study called 'Critical Race Theory.'

Marxism and Critical Theory contribute important building blocks to the ideological foundations of modern identity politics. Identity politics is rooted in the belief that society is fundamentally a power struggle between the oppressed and their societal oppressors.

And so, between Rousseau and Marx, we have some of the important foundations of the 'politics' in 'identity politics.'

4. Michael Foucault, Jean-François Lyotard and Postmodernism

Several important elements of identity politics also find their roots in the ideas and ideologies of postmodernism. Postmodernism developed in the late twentieth century through thinkers such as Michael Foucault and Jean-François Lyotard. It pushed back against the modernist Enlightenment ideas of rationality and objectivity, and instead saw truth claims as relative, as opposed to objective, and products of social conditioning. As Lyotard puts it, postmodernism expresses 'incredulity toward metanarratives' and sees knowledge as something that 'makes no claims to being original or even true... [and] should not be accorded predictive value in relation to reality, but strategic value in relation to the questions raised.'[10] Put simply, postmodernism denies the existence of objective truth; one person's truth can be different to another's.

In some ways, identity politics is an unsurprising product of a postmodern society which places greater value on subjective convictions than on objective truth-claims. In the modernistic framework, the most powerful and compelling claims about reality were those backed up by reason, evidence and science. In contrast, in the postmodern framework, the most powerful and compelling claims about reality are those backed up by personal conviction and people's subjective 'lived experiences.'

The influence of postmodernism can be seen across various aspects of identity politics. It can probably explain, at least in part, why the roll-out of unconscious bias training does not seem to have been deterred much by the lack of evidence for its effectiveness to change behaviour. But perhaps the most powerful example of postmodern influence is in the trans movement, which is driven by the principle that a person's subjective experience of gender identity is of far greater importance and significance than their biological sex. Even the phrase 'sex assigned at birth' (to refer to biological sex) implies that biological sex itself is not objective, but subjectively decided by midwives and/or parents.

Identity politics is intertwined with the postmodern idea that individuals' subjective convictions and experiences trump appeals to reason and evidence. If modernity and the Enlightenment form the era of 'facts don't care about your feelings,' postmodernity and identity politics could be seen as the era of 'feelings don't care about your facts.'

5. Social Media

We live in a virtual world. Social media has transformed how millions view reality and is altering the fabric of society in ways we are only beginning to understand. There are several ways social media has contributed to the rise of identity politics.

Firstly, social media has unprecedented power to raise awareness of moral atrocities being committed across the world. The murder of George Floyd was captured on a handful of mobile devices and then rapidly shared to screens across the globe. The #MeToo movement began following the sexual abuse revelations about Harvey Weinstein, but through social media, quickly became a global movement with millions of women publicly voicing that they too had been victims of sexual harassment and assault. The ubiquity of social media has enabled the raising of global awareness of these sorts of issues in ways previous generations could never have imagined.

Secondly, social media algorithms are designed to feed users with content that maintains their attention and encases them in echo chambers with people who share and reinforce their own views. This has facilitated identity groups uniting and communicating over previously insurmountable geographical barriers. Furthermore, it has allowed information and ideas to be rapidly propagated to the precisely relevant recipients all around the world, unfiltered and usually unhindered by governments and other regulators. In the 1930s Stella Browne had to tour the country to implore women to fight for their autonomy by joining the campaign for abortion rights. Today, the same message can be broadcasted to millions of receptive eyes and ears in seconds with a few taps of a phone screen.

Thirdly, social media is fertile soil for postmodern ideology. Postmodernism advocates for the creation and expression of our own subjective realities and identities. With social media, we can literally do just that. We can now create any identity profile we want for ourselves, and broadcast to the world any version of our reality that our imaginations can conjure up. This was encapsulated by an advert I came across for Instagram Reels. The advert pictured a woman applying colourful face paint and the attached slogan read: 'Make yourself in your own image. Explore who you can be with Reels. #YoursToMake.' If postmodernism says that we can decide our own reality based on our convictions, desires and experiences, then social media gives us the seemingly ideal soil in which this philosophy can take root.

6. Jesus and the God-Shaped Hole

Finally, as historian Tom Holland proposes in his book *Dominion*, from a historical perspective, Christianity has given the Western world many of its foundational moral values: from the equality of the sexes, to the upholding of universal human rights, to the duties of the welfare state, to the sanctity of monogamous marriage.[11]

However, as Friedrich Nietzsche foresaw, the West has now largely abandoned its Christian roots in exchange for a secular worldview.[12] This has led to an odd cultural paradox in which the West is distancing itself from the God of the Bible, whilst at the same time trying to retain, uphold and champion the very values it obtained from Christianity. In light of this, some secular commentators have argued that identity politics has arisen in an attempt to fill the God-shaped hole in Western society. For example, Douglas Murray argues that the 'explanations for our existence' that were provided by religion and politics have successively collapsed since the nineteenth century.[13] Murray then goes on: 'The question of what exactly we are meant to do now... was going to have to be answered by something. The answer that has presented itself in recent years is to engage in new battles, ever fiercer campaigns and ever more niche demands.'[13]

Author Tara Isabella Burton goes even further, arguing that identity politics still has the skeletal structures and language of the religion it is attempting to replace:

> Modern social justice culture has managed to create a thoroughly compelling, eschatologically focused account of a meaningful world, in which every human being has a fundamental purpose in a cosmic struggle, all without including, well, God... The social justice movement is so successful because it replicates the cornerstones of traditional religion- meaning, purpose, community, and ritual...[14]

There is much more to be said on this topic and so this idea, that identity politics is attempting to fill a God-shaped hole in society, is one we shall be returning to in Chapters 9 and 10 when we begin to formulate a Christian response to identity politics.

Who are the Oppressors?

Returning now to the grand metanarrative of identity politics, it is worth exploring who the protagonists are in the story. If identity politics is built on the framing of society as a power struggle between the oppressed and the oppressors, who are the oppressed and who are the oppressors?

We have spent the first four chapters of this book exploring the oppressed groups in this culture of identity politics. The oppressed are those who have experienced discrimination and disadvantage for centuries such as women, ethnic minorities, gay people, and trans people. Individuals who fall into more than one of these groups gain particular recognition as having experienced unique oppression. This is referred to as 'intersectionality.'

Who then are the oppressors? Naturally, the oppressor groups are usually viewed as the antheses of the oppressed groups: men, white people, heterosexuals, and cis-gendered people. However, on further reflection, several other characteristics are usually associated with the oppressor groups. Oppressors are also classically: politically conservative (people seemingly ideologically driven to maintain the status quo in society), middle-class (people who have benefitted economically from the status quo), and… Christian! In the story of identity politics, Christians have found themselves labelled as the oppressors – the homophobic, transphobic, sexist, racist, anti-liberal, anti-progressive, bigots who need to be overthrown.

For example in 2016, the US Commission on Civil Rights published a report titled 'Peaceful Coexistence: Reconciling Non-Discrimination Principles with Civil Liberties' in which they wrote:

the phrases "religious liberty" and "religious freedom" will stand for nothing except hypocrisy so long as they remain code words for discrimination, intolerance, racism, sexism, homophobia, Islamophobia, Christian supremacy or any other form of intolerance.[15]

Notice the presupposition here. Christian liberties and freedoms do not *risk becoming* discriminatory; they already are, and risk *remaining,* code words for bigotry.

These sorts of views have caught some Christians off-guard. A 2019 UK Foreign Office Report concluded that Christians are the most oppressed religious group in the world.[16] Furthermore, Christians have played instrumental roles in the histories of some of the social justice movements, from William Wilberforce and the Clapham Sect to Martin Luther King Junior. But now, Christians are generally seen as the oppressors – the bad guys in our cultural story.

Search Me and Know My Heart

Unsurprisingly, many Christians have not taken kindly to being labelled as the oppressors in the grand story of identity politics. Various attempts have been made to challenge and rebut this labelling, which will be our content for the next three chapters.

However, before we get there, it is paramount that we do not leave this chapter without acknowledging that Christians' hands are not entirely clean. The accusation of oppression is sadly not unfounded. Throughout history, Christians have been responsible for some horrendous acts of oppression and discrimination, from extensive involvement in the Transatlantic Slave Trade, to reprehensible intolerance towards individuals based on their gender or sexuality. There is much in church history that Christians should be ashamed of and that has legitimately brought the name of Jesus into disrepute.

Furthermore, in recent years the Evangelical Church has been rocked by several scandals in which it has been revealed that powerful, influential, and mostly male, church leaders have used their status and power to abuse, bully and oppress vulnerable people. And their victims were often those who were meant to be under their spiritual care. Detailed analysis and reflection on the recent church abuse scandals are, although vitally important, beyond the remit of this book. But the actions of abusive church leaders show us, beyond any doubt, that today's Church in general, and the Evangelical Church in particular, has been home to appalling cultures of oppression and abuses of power within its walls.

Closer to home, what about our church family? And what about our own hearts? When people enter our church doors who do not look, speak, or act like us, do we welcome them as precious brothers and sisters in Christ? Or is there discrimination and prejudice in our hearts, words and actions?

In his book *We Need to Talk About Race,* pastor Ben Linsday recounts several testimonies from black Christian women who have experienced cultures of prejudice in British churches. The testimonies are eye-opening; here is one excerpt from a woman called Vivienne:

> I have heard a lot of preaching and prayers asking God for a multicultural church, but I sometimes wonder if they really want or expect our prayers to be answered… because I have heard it said that we [black women] clap too loud and that we pray for too long. I have seen eyebrows raised, and music being played out loud in order to drown out the voice of the person who is praying.[17]

When we hear the accusation of oppression as Christians, our first response should not be defence, or even worse, attack. Rather, our first response should surely be repentance; and there is much repentance to be done. We all need to be ready and willing to pray with King David: 'Search me, God, and know my heart; test me and know my anxious thoughts. See if there is any offensive way in me, and lead me in the way everlasting' (Psalm

139:23-24). It is then, and only then, that we can begin to speak with any integrity about the good news of Jesus to our culture.

Conclusion

We have seen in this chapter that the identity politics movements are united by a grand narrative of the oppressed rising up to fight against and overthrow their societal oppressors. These ideas have their roots in a range of philosophies and ideologies that have shaped our modern culture. However, in this grand narrative, Christians have found themselves labelled as the oppressors who need to be overthrown. We will shortly be coming to how Christians have responded, and should respond, to this cultural story. But before we get there, we need to begin with repentance. We need to acknowledge the oppression and discrimination in our history, our churches, and our own hearts, and seek forgiveness both from God and from the world.

Part 2:
Three Common Christian Responses to Identity Politics

6. Mirror

'Identity politics... on the left... has stimulated the rise of identity politics on the right'
Francis Fukuyama, Identity

'Blessed are you when people insult you...'
Jesus, Matthew 5:11

In Part 1 of this book, we explored the stories of the identity politics revolution and the overarching metanarrative that tells of the oppressed groups in society rising up to fight against their oppressors. In this story of identity politics, Christians have found themselves in the role not of passive observers, nor protagonist heroes, nor victims of oppression, but rather as the villains – the bigoted oppressors who need to be overthrown.

Unsurprisingly, many Christians have taken issue with being labelled as the oppressors in this cultural narrative. Responses to identity politics have varied widely across cultures, theologies and personalities. In the next three chapters we are going to be exploring three of the most common responses faithful

Christians have had to identity politics: mirror, argue and ignore. As will become apparent, I suggest that all three have proven problematic. Then in Part 3, we will be looking at a potentially better way to speak for Jesus in this world of identity politics.

Mirror, Mirror

We begin this Part by exploring how some people have sought to respond to identity politics by mirroring the words, actions and campaigns of the social justice movements. Identity politics centres around the oppressed in society coalescing around their marginalised identity groups, such as being female, ethnic minority, gay or trans, and rising up to fight against their oppressors. One consequence of this social narrative has been a reactive and mirroring response from groups labelled as the oppressors – namely those who are white, male, straight, cis-gendered, middle-class, conservative and Christian. In response to the identity politics movements, some who fall into these oppressor categories have hunkered down into their own identity groups and begun to fight for their own rights and liberties that they perceive to be under attack. The retaliative strategy often involves taking the accusations, strategies and sometimes insults used by the social justice activists and levelling these straight back at them. Insults are repaid with similar insults and accusations are met with equivalent counteraccusations. And so, the battlelines are drawn for the so-called 'culture wars.' There is a variety of examples of this mirroring response across the spheres of identity politics.

You Took the Words Out of My Mouth

Positive discrimination in favour of women and ethnic minorities has always had its opponents. As we saw in Chapter 1, the introduction of all-women shortlists in the UK Labour Party led to some male politicians suing the party on grounds of discrimination against men. However, some have gone further and labelled positive discrimination as itself racist and/or sexist. For example, in 2014, Deputy Mayor of London Munira Mirza, who is a British Pakistani woman, appeared on BBC's *Daily Politics* to debate the place of positive discrimination in parliament. Mirza argued that success should be based on merit rather than on race or sex and concluded: 'You can't solve the racism or the sexism of the past by more racism and sexism.'[1]

The accusation of racism levelled at the racial justice movement can be seen elsewhere. As we mentioned in Chapter 2, journalist Douglas Murray described the teaching of 'Whiteness Studies' as 'a fairly good demonstration of racism.'[2]

The allegation of racism has also been levelled at the Black Lives Matter organisation as a whole. In July 2016, former Mayor of New York Rudy Giuliani (who later became part of President Donald Trump's legal team) appeared on CBS and said: 'When you say 'black lives matter' that is inherently racist. Black lives matter, white lives matter, Asian lives matter, Hispanic lives matter. That's anti-American, and it's racist.'[3] When Garry McCarthy, former superintendent of the Chicago Police Department, was asked in a CNN town hall meeting whether he agreed with Giuliani, McCarthy responded: 'Well I can tell you this, I think if there was a movement called 'white lives matter' it would be considered racist.'[4]

This mirroring of the phrase 'lives matter' has since been used more broadly by a range of campaigns against the Black Lives Matter movement. For example, in June 2020, the slogan 'white lives matter' made headlines in the UK following a football match between Manchester City FC and Burnley FC at the Etihad Stadium in Manchester. As the players and match officials took the knee in solidarity with Black Lives Matter, an aeroplane flew over the stadium dragging a large banner which read: 'White Lives Matter Burnley.' The banner was roundly condemned, including by Burnley FC who immediately released a press statement saying: 'Burnley Football Club strongly condemns the actions of those responsible for the aircraft and offensive banner that flew over The Etihad Stadium on Monday evening. We wish to make it clear that those responsible are not welcome at Turf Moor [Burnley's football stadium].'[5]

The man responsible for the flyby, Jake Hepple, defended his actions to the *Mail Online*, saying: 'I'm not racist... We were not trying to offend the movement or black people. I believe that it's also important to acknowledge that white lives matter too.'[6] Hepple was soon fired by his engineering firm.

Away from the racial justice movement, elements of this mirroring response to the identity politics campaigns can also be seen in other areas. We explored in Chapter 3 that the accusation of 'phobia' has been exchanged between those in favour and those opposed to Stonewall's Trans-Inclusivity Policy. Supporters of Stonewall such as the Labour Campaign for Trans Rights have labelled the LGB Alliance (the group that broke away from Stonewall over the issue of trans-inclusivity) as 'transphobic.'[7] In return LGB Alliance advocates such as their co-founder Kate Harris have branded Stonewall as 'homophobic.'[8]

This kind of polemical name-calling is now fairly common across the identity politics campaigns. Many social justice activists label their opponents as bigoted, phobic and dangerous, as well using more specific terms such as 'TERF' (trans-exclusionary radical feminist). In return, opponents of the identity politics movements level counter-insults such as 'snowflake' (referring to campaigners who are too fragile to face criticism) or 'liberal elite' (referring to people who claim to be on the side of the oppressed and working classes, but are actually part of the oppressive ruling classes). Even the word 'woke' which, as we saw in Chapter 5, originated in Black American folk music, is now sometimes used as an insult to disparage social justice campaigners.

And so, as the language and tactics of the social justice campaigners get mirrored and thrown back at them by their opponents, the world of identity politics turns into the world of culture wars.

Identity Politics Meets Politics

Several social commentators have now pointed out that this mirroring response to the identity politics movements is beginning to have significant impacts on domestic and international politics. As opposing identity groups draw their mirroring battlelines, political debate becomes increasingly polarised.

In his book *Identity,* author and political scientist Francis Fukuyama suggests that one of the most important and potentially problematic impacts of 'identity politics as currently practiced on the left is that it has stimulated the rise of identity politics on the right. Identity politics gives rise to political correctness, opposition to which has become a major course of mobilization on the right.'[9]

Fukuyama argues that the rise of politically liberal movements such as Fourth Wave Feminism and Black Lives Matter has led to a reactive, mirroring rise in the popularity of politically conservative groups and leaders, particularly amongst those labelled as oppressors. Fukuyama then goes on to suggest that this mirroring response from those on the political right, to the identity politics movements of the left, contributed (at least in part) to one of the biggest political surprises in recent years: the election of President Donald Trump in 2016. Fukuyama notes:

> ...many of Donald Trump's working-class supporters feel they have been disregarded by the national elites. Hollywood makes movies with strong female, black or gay characters, but few centering around people like themselves, except occasionally to make fun of them.[9]

Trump's messages of 'America First' and 'Make America Great Again' tapped into the desire of some white, conservative

Americans to have their identities valued, recognised and represented in politics, particularly in a culture which labels such people as the oppressors. This anti-establishment galvanising of ordinary, disillusioned citizens is sometimes referred to as 'populism.'

Of course, Trump has not been the only populist politician who has gained ascendency in recent years. The last few years have seen the rise of several right-wing populist parties across Europe such as the National Rally (formally called the National Front) in France, The Party for Freedom in the Netherlands, and the Alternative for Germany party.

Also in 2016, the UK voted via referendum to leave the European Union. The Brexit debate involved a range of different political, social and economic issues that we do not have the space to unpick here. Those who voted for Brexit did so for a wide variety of reasons. However, the themes of national identity, sovereignty and recognition of ordinary white working-class citizens, ran through many of the campaigns and slogans such as 'take back control' and 'believe in Britain.' As Fukuyama summarises: 'Britain's unexpected vote to leave the European Union in June 2016 was predicted to have disastrous economic consequences, but the issue for many Leave voters was one of identity rather than economics.'[9]

My purpose here is not to pass comment on those who voted for or against Trump, Brexit or any of the other political parties mentioned. Rather, it is simply to point out that this mirroring response to identity politics is having major consequences in the political arena, as different identity groups strive for recognition in this world shaped by the culture wars.

The Church and the Culture Wars

But of course, this mirroring response is not confined to activists and politicians who wish to make headlines and win votes. As Christians find themselves labelled as the oppressors in the narrative of identity politics, elements of this mirroring response are becoming gradually more noticeable within the Church.

Terms such as 'liberal elite' and 'woke' are now making their way into Sunday sermons, and there are broader calls for the Church in general, and the Evangelical Church in particular, to fight against the identity politics movements.

The Pew Research Centre reported that in the 2020 US Presidential Election, around 85 per cent of white evangelical protestants voted for Donald Trump making them one of Trump's most loyal demographic voting bases.[10] One of the most influential voices in American evangelicalism is theologian and pastor John MacArthur. In a podcast interview in August 2020, MacArthur publicly threw his support behind Trump, recalling a conversation in which he told Trump personally: 'From a biblical standpoint Christians could not vote Democratic... Any real true believer is going to be on your side in this election.'[11]

Around a month later, a clip of MacArthur's sermon from Grace Community Church in California was uploaded to YouTube, in which MacArthur preached:

> And then there are the social anarchists, the protesters and the rioters who are trying to reset society to their will by fear and anarchy... They create chaos for chaos' sake: looting, shooting, killing those who they view as oppressors or capitalists. They are after a scorched world, that they can redo in godless immoral socialism.[12]

Elements of the mirroring response to identity politics can be seen in MacArthur's words here. MacArthur blames social justice campaigners of sewing fear and anarchy, and he describes their goals as immoral. But more notably, he accuses protesters of shooting and killing innocent people. Without wanting to overly postulate MacArthur's intentions, this seems to be language specifically chosen, not merely to oppose the social justice movements, but to mirror the accusations made by Black Lives Matter protesters against the US police force.

But this mirroring response from Christians is not just verbal. There have been some prominent actions and campaigns from Christian groups that bear a notable resemblance to the campaigns, and in particular the boycotts, of the social justice movements.

The Southern Baptist Convention (SBC) is an association of Baptist churches in the US which was founded in 1845 and has since grown to a membership of around fourteen million people in over 47,000 churches. In June 1997, at their annual convention gathering, the SBC voted to begin a boycott of the Walt Disney Company. The reasons for SBC's boycott were Disney's employee policy which accepted gay relationships on insurance plans, and the release of the 1994 film Priest whose protagonist was a gay Roman Catholic priest. The convention resolution read: 'Southern Baptists give serious and prayerful reconsideration to their purchase and support of Disney products and to boycott the Disney Company and theme parks if they continue this anti-Christian and anti-family trend.'[13]

The boycott of the entire Disney empire, including films, TV channels, theme parks, shops and merchandise lasted eight years before the SBC eventually voted to end its boycott in 2005.

Does the Mirror Work?

This chapter has so far explored how some individuals and organisations, who have been labelled as oppressors in the narrative of identity politics, have responded by mirroring the language and actions of the social justice campaigners. There is a significant group of people, including some influential church leaders and Christian organisations, who have responded to the identity politics movements by hunkering down into their own identity groups, drawing the battlelines of the culture wars, and levelling the language and strategies of the social justice activists straight back at them.

So is mirroring a good response to identity politics? I would suggest that it is not, for at least three reasons.

1. Mirroring Alienates Listeners

Firstly, mirroring alienates people who already think Christians are undesirable bigots. Most Christians feel understandably hurt, offended and potentially enraged if we get accused of sexism, racism or bigotry, whether or not these accusations are true (and as we saw in Chapter 5, they sometimes are). Therefore, it is surely predictable that Christians will meet animosity if we start levelling these accusations back at our accusers. If we start calling social justice activists 'racist' or 'snowflakes,' we should not be surprised if they then do not want to darken the doors of our churches.

That is not to say that we should not debate and challenge those who oppose the Bible's teaching. We will be exploring this in more detail in the next chapter. But if we want to engage with those around us, and share the good news of Jesus with them, it seems illogical that we would start by insulting our opponents, particularly in ways that we know from experience to be upsetting and offensive.

2. Mirroring Escalates Tensions

Linked to this, it would appear that this mirroring response has contributed to the escalation of already volatile political situations through the deepening of divisions between identity groups. Over the last few years, as social justice movements and populist right-wing groups have both gained popularity, political discourse has become more polarised and more hostile. In 2014, a Pew Research survey found that amongst both Democrats and Republicans in the US, those who hold a 'highly negative' view of the other party have more than doubled since 1994.[14] The study also found that 27 per cent of Democrats view the Republican party as a 'threat to the nation's well-being' and

36 per cent of Republicans think exactly the same about the Democratic Party.[14]

However, this polarisation of political discourse is having consequences beyond the ballot box. As politics becomes increasingly polarised, productive political debate quickly turns into abusive mudslinging. But even more tragically, hostile words have too often turned into hostile actions. In the last few years, we have had news cycles filled with violent and sometimes deadly clashes, particularly between Trump supporters and social justice campaigners such as those associated with Black Lives Matter. According to data from the Armed Conflict Location and Event Data project, in the year 2020, at least twenty-five Americans were killed during political protests or other political unrest in the US.[15]

Clearly, those who perpetrate violence need to be held accountable for their own actions. But in light of statistics like these, it surely is incumbent on society at large to try to deescalate tensions and calm the volatility of political discourse wherever possible, rather than escalating tensions through mirroring the insults of our accusers.

3. Mirroring is not Christ-Like

We have so far seen that mirroring can alienate those who already think of Christians as bigots and escalate already volatile political situations. However, the third and most important reason why mirroring is problematic is because it is not how Jesus taught us to act.

One of the repeated themes in Jesus' Sermon on the Mount in Matthew 5-7 is how we should respond when those around us accuse and insult us. In Matthew 5:11-12, Jesus preaches:

> Blessed are you when people insult you, persecute you and falsely say all kinds of evil against you because of me. Rejoice and be glad, because great is your reward in

heaven, for in the same way they persecuted the prophets who were before you.

Accusations and insults simply for being a follower of God are nothing new. As Jesus points out, it has been the experience God's people since the time of the Old Testament prophets. In fact, Jesus makes the paradoxical declaration that it is actually those who are accused and insulted because of Him who are 'blessed' – recipients of God's favour in this life and His reward in the next.

Jesus then goes on, a few verses later in Matthew 5:38-48:

> You have heard that it was said, 'Eye for eye, and tooth for tooth.' But I tell you, do not resist an evil person. If anyone slaps you on the right cheek, turn to them the other cheek also. And if anyone wants to sue you and take your shirt, hand over your coat as well…

> …I tell you, love your enemies and pray for those who persecute you, that you may be children of your Father in heaven. He causes his sun to rise on the evil and the good, and sends rain on the righteous and the unrighteous. If you love those who love you, what reward will you get? Are not even the tax collectors doing that? And if you greet only your own people, what are you doing more than others? Do not even pagans do that? Be perfect, therefore, as your heavenly Father is perfect.

Jesus paints an image of radical forgiveness for acts as offensive and humiliating as being slapped in the face or being sued for your shirt. But rather than retaliating to this persecution, Jesus says we are to love our enemies and pray for those who persecute us. As is often pointed out, Jesus went on to practice what He preached as He hung on the cross praying: 'Father forgive them, for they do not know what they are doing' (Luke 23:34). Jesus then emphasises the counter-cultural nature of this forgiveness by pointing out that loving and forgiving those who love us back is easy; even the corrupt tax-collectors and idolatrous pagans can do that. As C. S. Lewis puts it in *Mere Christianity*: 'Everyone says forgiveness is a lovely idea, until they have something to forgive.'[16] Instead, Christians have the high calling of displaying the perfect and unconditional love and forgiveness of God, even to those who reject us and Him.

That is not to say that there isn't a place for debating, criticising or indeed rebuking others; Jesus did plenty of all three. There are certainly times when we should call out hypocrisy and challenge those who oppose the Bible's teaching. But when we are insulted and offended, we should not *retaliate*. We should not, in the words of 1 Peter 3:9, 'repay... insult with insult.' We are called to turn the other cheek and love our accusers, not to verbally slap them back.

Conclusion

The first common response to identity politics that we have explored is 'mirroring.' Some opponents to the social justice movements, including some prominent Christians, have fought back against the identity politics narrative by taking the insults and accusations levelled by the social justice activists and throwing these straight back at them. So, we end up with the culture wars.

However, mirroring alienates those who already see Christians as bigots and has the potential to escalate a political environment that is already volatile. But most importantly, it is not how Jesus taught us to act. Rather than retaliating against our accusers by levelling their insults and accusations back at them, we are called to radical forgiveness and love towards our accusers. Instead of mirroring the words and actions of identity politics culture, Christians are commanded to mirror the love and forgiveness of the God who, despite our rejection of Him, first loved and forgave us.

7. Argue

'If liberty means anything at all, it means the right to tell people what they do not want to hear'
George Orwell, Freedom of the Press

'We can not allow hatred and intolerance to go unchallenged by anyone including by religious groups'
Joe Anderson (Mayor of Liverpool), on Twitter

When I was a teenager, I was given a DVD titled *The God Delusion Debate*. It was the recording of the 2007 debate between the Christian Professor of Mathematics John Lennox, and the atheist Professor of Evolutionary Biology Richard Dawkins, at the University of Alabama.[1] In the nearly two-hour long event the two professors debated the issues of God, science and rationality, loosely following the structure of Dawkins' bestselling book *The God Delusion*.[2] The event became one of the most famous and watched religious debates in recent history and has reached over 1.3 million views on YouTube. At the time, Dawkins was one of a group of increasingly prominent individuals who were publishing popular books defending the worldview of atheism and arguing that belief in God is irrational and unscientific. This group became known as the 'New Atheists' and included neuroscientist Sam Harris, philosopher Daniel Dennett and the late journalist Christopher Hitchens.

As I watched *The God Delusion Debate* for the first time in my childhood bedroom, I found that a lot of the discussion was far above my GCSE-level understanding of biology and mathematics. Nonetheless, I was captivated. It was the first time I had heard an intellectual defence for Christian faith, and it led me down a road that eventually resulted in me becoming convinced of the truth of Christianity and committing my life to Jesus.

There are several Christians who have tried to respond to identity politics culture in the same way that John Lennox responded to Richard Dawkins and the New Atheists – by tackling their arguments head-on in public, intellectual debate. This is our second common Christian response to identity politics: argue.

The Battle of Ideas

As Part 1 of this book set out, the roots of identity politics are a complex and wide-reaching web of different sociological, political, philosophical and theological ideas. It is therefore perhaps unsurprising that many of the foundational ideas of identity politics, such as Critical Theory and intersectionality, originated from, or were popularised on, university campuses- places designed to be melting pots for ideas and debate.

As we also saw throughout Part 1, there is a wide range of tricky questions and debates that identity politics is raising, and there is often disagreement within the movements themselves. Here are some of the debates we have already encountered in previous chapters:

- What is a woman? Does being a woman have any relation to anatomy or chromosomes, or is it solely based on how someone self-identifies?
- Is it racist to brand all white people as privileged and complicit in systemic racism?
- Does positive discrimination increase equality, or just discriminate against different groups?
- Should we still roll out unconscious bias training even if there is no strong evidence that it changes behaviour?
- Should children who make homophobic or racist remarks at nursery or school be investigated for extremism?
- Can retailers of products (such as personalised cakes) be compelled to print slogans they disagree with?
- Is holding conservative Christian views on marriage and sex compatible with being a politically liberal parliamentarian?
- Is using gender-neutral language such as 'bodies with vaginas' or 'chest-feeding' inclusive to trans people or demeaning to women (or both)?
- Are puberty blockers safe to be giving to children? And do children have enough cognitive capacity to understand the risks and consequences involved?
- How many genders are there? Two? Over a hundred? Somewhere in between?
- Is it fair to label Christians as 'oppressors' when they are one of the most oppressed religious groups in the world?

Perhaps disappointingly to some readers, I am not going to attempt to answer all, or indeed any, of these questions. I am sure there will be a diversity of views amongst readers on most, if not all, of these issues. However, we ought to at least agree that these are reasonable questions that are worth discussing and debating. Identity politics raises a plethora of tricky questions that deserve some time for consideration.

However, there is one major problem with engaging identity politics through debate.

Cancel Culture

The problem is that if you try to debate the issues raised by identity politics, or argue with the identity politics narrative, you quickly run headlong into so-called 'cancel culture.' One of the most challenging features of identity politics is that there is a narrow set of socially acceptable or 'politically correct' beliefs. If someone publicly expresses or even suggests any view that falls outside the range of 'politically correct' opinions, they run the high risk of being 'cancelled': being de-platformed, blocked on Twitter, called a bigot and then ignored. There is little room for debate or disagreement.

There are many examples we could discuss here and so what follows is just a selection of recent illustrations of cancel culture in action.

Cancel Culture in the Public Arena

Some of those who have felt the force of cancel culture are those who have actively sought to swim against the tide of the identity politics narrative.

We have already seen what happened when Germaine Greer took on her critics at the University of Cardiff. When campaigners accused Greer of 'continually misgendering trans women and denying the existence of transphobia altogether'[3] and tried her to get dis-invited from giving her 'Women and Power' lecture, Greer fought back. In an interview with BBC News, Greer doubled down on her views, saying:

> Apparently people have decided that because I don't think that post-operative transgender men (i.e., MtF transgender people) are women, I'm not to be allowed to talk… I'm not saying that people should not be allowed to go through that procedure. What I'm saying is that

it does not make them a woman. It happens to be an opinion.[4]

As we saw in Chapter 1, despite a vocal campaign to cancel her, Greer managed to deliver the lecture.

Someone else who pushed back against the identity politics narrative, but who, unlike Greer, *was* successfully cancelled is Prof. Kenneth Zucker. Zucker is Professor of Psychiatry at the University of Toronto and used to be psychologist-in-chief at the Toronto Centre for Addiction and Mental Health (CAMH). He is also the editor of the *Archives of Sexual Behaviour* journal, and in 2008, was appointed chairman of the American Psychiatric Association's workgroup on Sexual and Gender Identity Disorders. Despite this impressive academic and clinical CV, in 2015 Zucker was abruptly fired by CAMH and his gender identity clinic was shut down.

Zucker's dismissal came after mounting pressure from campaigners and a petition to 'Eliminate Dr. Kenneth Zucker' reached over 2000 signatures. The petition website accused Zucker of 'dehumanizing practices include teaching transgender children to be more content with their biological gender' and failing 'to see is that sex and gender are two separate entities.'[5] The petition also accused Zucker of breaking Ontario state laws that banned LGBTQ+ conversion therapies.[6] In an interview with *National Post*, Zucker defended his practices saying: 'We are trying to help a child feel more comfortable with the gender identity that matches their birth sex. That way, you are lowering the odds that as such a kid gets older, he or she will... require treatment with hormones and sex-reassignment surgery.'[7]

In February 2015, CAMH commissioned an external review into Zucker and his gender identity clinic. The review did not conclude that Zucker had been carrying out conversion therapies. However, it did criticise the clinic for being 'overly-conservative' in its slowness to refer children for hormonal therapies, and described the focus on psychotherapy to treat children's anxiety as 'outdated.'[8] Following Zucker's firing, CAMH's Child, Youth and Family Program Medical Director Kwame McKenzie issued an apology for Zucker's work, saying: 'We want to apologize for the fact that not all of the practices in our childhood gender identity clinic are in step with the latest thinking.'[9]

Greer and Zucker are two of numerous examples of public figures who have swum against the tide of identity politics and felt the force of cancel culture.

Cancel Culture and the Church

In addition, there have been several notable examples of cancel culture successfully bringing down Christians who have caught the attention of the social justice activists.

As we explored in Chapter 3, the large American fast-food chain Chick-fil-A was driven out of business in the UK by campaigners who took issue with the company donating money to organisations that allegedly opposed LGBTQ+ rights: namely the Salvation Army and the Fellowship of Christian Athletes. Chick-fil-A was founded by Samuel Truett Cathy who was a committed Christian and member of the First Baptist Church. Today, the company still keeps to some of Cathy's Christian ethos, such as not opening on a Sunday to allow employees to rest and attend church.[10] Those who created the petition to close down the UK branches of Chick-fil-A did not accuse the company of making any homophobic comments or discriminating against gay customers or employees.[11] For Chick-fil-A, it was simply being a company with a Christian ethos, that donated money to Christian charities such as the Salvation Army, that was enough to get them cancelled and driven out of the UK.

In 2020, another famous Christian name met the force of cancel culture. *Premier Christianity* magazine published an article in December 2019 titled '2020: The Year of Evangelism.'[12] The article optimistically predicted that 2020 could be a year of major gospel revival in the UK, as 'across churches and denominations, age groups and genders, there's a fresh sense that 2020 could be a year when God acts, powerfully.'[12] One of the leading reasons the article gave for this optimism was that the UK was anticipating the arrival of the evangelist Franklin Graham. Franklin Graham is the son of Billy Graham and is currently the president and CEO of the Billy Graham Evangelistic Association. In 2020, Franklin Graham was set to do a large, eight-city preaching tour of the UK, with stops at the Birmingham Arena, Glasgow SSE Hydro, Liverpool M&S Arena, and the final event at The O2 in London. However, 2020 did not pan out in the way Franklin Graham or *Premier Christianity* anticipated, for several reasons.

Graham began to draw criticism in the UK due to his vocal support for President Trump and his belief that homosexuality is a sin – a view that he has reiterated multiple times on social media. A petition to ban Graham from the UK gained over 8,000 signatures, and several MPs including a government minister reportedly urged the Home Secretary to refuse him entry into the country. As a result of this mounting pressure from campaigners, all eight of Graham's booked venues cancelled his events. Following the cancellation of the event at the M&S Arena in Liverpool, Mayor of Liverpool Joe Anderson posted on Twitter: 'Our City is a diverse City and proud of our LGBTQ+ community and always will be. We can not allow hatred and intolerance to go unchallenged by anyone including by religious groups or sects. It's right we have banned from the M&S Arena Franklin Graham.'

Graham hit back at his opponents in an interview with Religion News Service, saying: 'This attack on me is an attack on religious freedom and freedom of speech.'[13] He announced that he would still be coming to the UK and was organising a set of alternative venues. However, Graham's revised plans were then halted by the COVID-19 pandemic.

Over the ensuing two years, Graham engaged in a series of legal battles against the venues that cancelled him. Finally in

2022, Graham successfully made it to the UK and completed a smaller tour of four cities in England and Wales.

But it is not just large corporations and outspoken evangelists that have been felled by cancel culture. There have also been several lesser-known Christians who have experienced the power of cancel culture for holding beliefs contrary to the prevailing narrative of identity politics. One notable example is Felix Ngole.

Felix Ngole was a Masters student studying Social Work at the University of Sheffield. In September 2015, Ngole posted a series of comments on Facebook which included quotes from Leviticus 18:22 and Romans 1:26-28, along with comments including 'same sex marriage is a sin whether we accept it or not' and 'homosexuality is a sin, no matter how you want to dress it up.' Following a 'fitness to practice' investigation into Ngole and his Facebook posts, he was expelled from Sheffield University.

However, Ngole fought back and in 2017, brought legal action against the university. The High Court ruled against Ngole, judging that the University had acted lawfully in expelling Ngole due to the university's 'responsibilities to play their part in guaranteeing carefulness and high standards in the social work profession he wanted to join, in the interests of vulnerable service users and of the wider public.'[14]

Ngole then brought the case to the Court of Appeal, and in 2019 the Court of Appeal overturned the ruling from the High Court, stating that the expulsion of Ngole was unfair and disproportionate, and that 'the University wrongly confused the expression of religious views with the notion of discrimination.'[15] Following the ruling from the Court of Appeal the Chief Executive of the Christian Legal Centre Andrea Williams commented:

> We are delighted that the Court of Appeal has… made a ruling that accords with common sense… We hope this sends out a message of freedom across all universities and professions that Christians and others should be

allowed to express their views without fear of censorship
or discipline.[16]

But despite the optimism of Williams and others, censorship
is undoubtably increasing in today's culture of identity politics.
Expressing, or even suggesting, politically incorrect views leads
to the high risk of being cancelled, if not by laws and institutions,
then by petitions and social media storms.

Outside the BBC's Broadcasting House in central London
stands a statue of the author George Orwell. On the wall beside
him is inscribed the quotation from Orwell: 'If liberty means
anything at all, it means the right to tell people what they do not
want to hear.'[17] However, today 'liberty' is not associated with
free speech and robust debate. Rather it is defined by cancel
culture and intolerance towards all politically incorrect opinions.
Ironically, this is all done in the name of 'tolerance.'

What Now for Evangelism?

How then can Christians engage with a culture that moves to
cancel anyone who expresses a 'politically incorrect' belief?
We shall be giving a much more comprehensive answer to this
question in Part 3 of this book. However, one response that is
becoming decreasingly effective is arguing.

The global Church owes a huge debt of gratitude to John
Lennox and other Christian apologists who were willing to
take on the ideas and arguments of Richard Dawkins and the
New Atheists, in the public square and at the highest levels of
academic debate. When Dawkins claimed that 'faith is the great
cop-out, the great excuse to evade the need to think and evaluate
evidence,'[18] it required a response from those who could show
that it is not.

Despite the opposing worldviews of Lennox and Dawkins,
the reason why these two professors could even participate in a
debate with each other is because both hold to the modernistic
beliefs of objective truth and the authority of reason, logic and

evidence. *The God Delusion Debate* would have quickly unravelled if one of them held to the postmodern belief that there is no objective truth!

But in recent years, our culture has shifted away from the modernistic beliefs in the primacy of science and reason, and towards the postmodern beliefs that truth is relative and personal conviction is of primary authority. Therefore, in this postmodern culture, those who hold views that disagree with the prevailing culture meet opposition not through debate and argumentation, but dismissal and cancellation. This is particularly true for those who are straight, white, cisgendered and male. Falling into these categories means proponents are seen as not possessing the relevant 'lived experience' that validates their place in public discourse. And so, they are a prime target for cancel culture.

Clearly, there are still many debates that are worth having and questions that are worth raising in all the different areas of identity politics, as we saw at the start of this chapter. Therefore, Christians ought to be strongly defending and upholding the legitimate place for debate and disagreement in public discourse, especially in the university setting. However, I do also fear that if Christians continue to reach for arguments as our primary tool with which we engage with identity politics, we will find ourselves increasing being brought down by cancel culture and losing our place in the public square. It often does not matter if our points are logical or our beliefs are true; if they are politically incorrect, they run the high risk of being cancelled.

Conclusion

There are some Christians and church leaders who have instinctively responded to identity politics in the same way that apologists took on the ideas of the New Atheists- by tackling their arguments head-on in the public arena, with reason, logic and facts. There are, after all, many debates worth having and questions worth raising, such as 'Is positive discrimination really fair?' or 'Are puberty blockers really safe to be giving to children?'

However, in our postmodern culture, publicly expressing any view that falls outside the range of 'politically correct' opinions leads to the high risk of being cancelled and de-platformed. There appears to be little room for debate on these issues in modern public discourse.

As we shall explore in Part 3, perhaps it is time for a new type of apologetics.

8. Ignore

'Keep Calm and Carry On'
British Government, WWII poster

'For I am not ashamed of the gospel…'
Apostle Paul, Romans 1:16

So far, we have looked at how some Christians have responded to identity politics by mirroring the language and campaigns of the social justice activists, whilst others have tried to debate and argue the issues raised by these movements. However, we have so far not mentioned what I think is the most common Christian response to identity politics: just ignore it. Many Christians are simply too fearful to broach the topics of race, feminism or gender in public, or indeed in private, and so they simply bury their heads in the sand. Preachers carry on doing the same talks, sermons and carol services that they have been doing for the past half century. And when ordinary Christians encounter these topics in conversations at the water-cooler, school-gate or pub, many just keep their head down and wait for the danger to pass.

Billy Graham Comes to the UK

We began this book by travelling back to the 1950s and the first time Billy Graham touched down in the UK to preach at Haringey Arena. Hundreds of thousands of Brits flocked to hear the young American evangelist preach the gospel, and night after night, thousands publicly committed to following Jesus. Theologian J. I. Packer described the first Billy Graham Haringey Crusade as 'by far the most momentous religious event in 20th-century Britain.'[1]

One of the remarkable aspects of Graham's preaching was how simple and straight his gospel messages were. The former Rector of All Souls Church Langham Place, Richard Bewes, was twenty years old when Graham arrived in the UK. Bewes recalled: 'He [Graham] disdained high flowering oratory, complicated metaphors or many jokes. He spoke with gravity, and seriousness about our need and God's solution.'[2] Pastor Craig Brian Lawson described Graham's sermons saying: 'He majored in the gospel in a way simple and clear, [and] relied on Scripture alone for his authority- repeating "the Bible says" without apology.'[3] Graham preached simple and unashamed messages of sin, salvation and repentance, and thousands responded to his call.

But arguably Graham's even greater legacy than those who came to faith at his Crusades, was the countless number of Christians who were inspired by Graham to preach and teach the gospel in their communities across the country and world. John Stott, who became a friend and colleague of Graham said of Graham: 'He did much... to encourage younger evangelists. He put evangelism on the ecclesiastical map, making it respectable in a new way.'[4] Richard Bewes was one such minister who was inspired by Graham, recalling that the Crusades were 'a landmark time in my life and for a number who were called into ministry at that time.'[2]

Graham blazed a trail that many evangelists and churches then followed, and today, we can see Graham's fingerprints all over our evangelistic talks, sermons and events. Like Graham's sermons, many of our evangelistic messages begin with a Bible passage, springboard off into a summary of sin, salvation, repentance and eternal life, and then end on an altar call or prayer of repentance.

However, there is one thing that has changed since Billy Graham's UK Crusade in 1954: the audience.

It's Not Like The Old Days

In his book *Honest Evangelism*, evangelist and author of the Christianity Explored course Rico Tice describes how the UK's response to the gospel has changed since the 1950s:

> When the American evangelist Billy Graham came to the UK for the first time in 1954, he packed out stadiums night after night... By the time I joined the staff at All Souls Langham Place in central London in 1994, the culture was hardening against Christianity... Today [writing in 2015], people are on a totally different road... Culturally, we're such a long way from biblical Christianity that people don't object to faith having engaged with it; they just simply dismiss it.[5]

Identity politics has caused a seismic shift, not only in how our culture operates, but also in how it responds to the message of Jesus. In the 1950s and 60s the gospel was seen, at least by the thousands who fell to their knees in repentance in Haringey Arena, as good news of great joy for all people. In the early 2000s the gospel was seen, at least by the thousands who read and followed the writings and arguments of the New Atheists, as an irrational fairy-story for the intellectually naïve. But today the gospel is seen, at least by the thousands who have been captivated and galvanised by the identity politics movements, as the oppressive edits of a bygone era that need to be silenced and overthrown.

We perhaps have the starkest illustration of this societal shift when we compare how the UK responded to Billy Graham in the 1950s, to how it responded to his son, Franklin Graham, in 2020. In the 1950s, Billy Graham flew to the UK and thousands came out to hear and respond to the gospel. In 2020, Franklin Graham tried to come to the UK and all of his booked venues cancelled him.

Keep Calm and Carry On

Despite this seismic shift in the way that our culture responds to the gospel, which has occurred within a single generation, many Christians seem content to simply carry on as normal. Identity politics has radically changed how the Church and the gospel are viewed by our culture, and yet many churches have chosen to ignore the revolution happening on their doorsteps and carry on doing the same Billy Graham-style evangelistic talks that they have been doing for the last fifty years. In the words of the poster that the British government published in the run up to World War II, and that has since become a ubiquitous internet meme, many Christians have chosen to just 'Keep Calm and Carry On.'

There appears to be at least two major reasons why a significant proportion of Christians are ignoring the ways that identity politics is altering how our culture responds to Christians and the gospel.

Firstly, it is genuinely difficult to keep up with an identity politics culture that, in historical terms, has appeared nearly overnight. The campaigns, language, ideologies and policies of the different social justice movements are constantly changing and evolving. Therefore understandably, many Christians do not see it as a high priority to keep up to date with the latest legal battles or Twitter storms. Social media also exacerbates this. As mentioned in Chapter 5, social media encases users in echo chambers with others that affirm and reinforce their pre-existing beliefs. Therefore, it is foreseeable that Christian social media users can end up in echo chambers that shield them from the views of those who disagree with them.

Secondly, and probably more powerfully, many Christians ignore the identity politics movements out of fear. After all, who would volunteer to be the next Felix Ngole or Chick-fil-A? When we see people losing jobs, opportunities and reputations for pushing back against identity politics culture, the natural and understandable response is to keep our mouths shut and try to blend into the background. Most people do not have the money, resources or will to fight freedom-of-speech cases in court, or to risk losing jobs or businesses over social media posts. We keep calm and carry on because to do anything else would be too risky.

Is Ignorance Bliss?

However, I would suggest that there are three main reasons why this response, of ignoring identity politics, is problematic.

1. The Times Have Changed

Firstly, as is becoming increasingly recognised, our evangelistic sermons are generally not landing like they used to.

In his book *Evangelism in a Sceptical World,* Australian evangelist Sam Chan writes:

> At some stage in the last few decades, we moved away from foundationalist reasoning. And we became suspicious of metanarratives and claims of ultimate truth. We moved away from the age of modernity into the age of postmodernity. The methods of evangelism that once worked so well in the 1980s no longer had the same appeal in the 2000s.[6]

Rico Tice says something similar in *Honest Evangelism*:

> The days when you could go from zero to the gospel in a single conversation are not the norm- keep praying for it, but don't be discouraged by it not happening. It's very rare for someone to meet a Christian, come to a guest service the next month, and then sign up for a Christianity Explored- type course.[5]

To be clear, I still think there is an important place for Billy Graham-style evangelistic talks. People continue to come to faith through the preaching of straight, expositional, evangelistic sermons. Furthermore, during the lockdowns of the COVID-19 pandemic, the UK Church saw a huge spike in those interested in hearing Bible teaching. Some churches had hundreds, and sometimes thousands, more people tune into their online church services than would normally walk through the doors on a Sunday. In addition, some evangelistic courses such as Christianity Explored saw a surge in sign-ups when they went online. Clearly God can and does work through straight, expositional evangelistic sermons today.

But at the same time, it is undoubtably becoming increasingly difficult to draw unbelievers into churches in order to hear a Bible talk. Even the act of preaching itself, especially if done by a white, middle-class, middle-aged man, is seen by some as the epitome of oppressive patriarchy. Outside the church building, in the public square, evangelism is arguably even more challenging, as speakers who hold 'politically incorrect' beliefs are finding it increasingly difficult to simply secure a platform – and that is before they try to fill the auditorium.

Gone are the days when charismatic evangelists can pack out UK stadiums by preaching straight gospel messages. It would appear that the days of filling lecture theatres and church pews with non-Christians who are willing to give the gospel a fair hearing are also probably beginning to fade into history. Is it really adequate to ignore the social revolution happening in our culture and continue doing the same evangelistic talks and events that we have been doing for the last fifty years?

2. The Elephant is in the Room

Secondly, we cannot ignore identity politics because it is already impacting and shaping the Church.

If our churches were demographically representative of the UK population (and admittedly this is almost never the case), then in our congregations, 14 per cent of people would be non-white,[7] 3 per cent would be gay, lesbian or bisexual,[8] 0.4 per cent would be trans,[9] and of course roughly half would be women. Therefore, there are large proportions of our church congregations who have probably experienced the kinds of discrimination and prejudice that the social justice movements are focussed on addressing. So it should not surprise us to find Christians who are attracted to and influenced by the social justice movements. Identity politics is not some isolated philosophy that is being propagated in a distant land. The ideas and ideologies of the social justice movements directly pertain to and impact a large proportion of our church congregations.

Furthermore, identity politics is beginning to shape church culture and church policy-making. This is not always a bad thing. As we saw in Chapter 5, the Church has been home to appalling acts of discrimination, oppression and abuse of power, both historically and in the modern day. Where identity politics shines a light on church practices that are oppressive, discriminatory or in any other way sinful, we should be grateful for the wake-up call and committed to repentance. However, there are also some aspects of the identity politics movements that jar with Christian beliefs (more on this in the next two chapters). As with every era in history from the birth of the Church, there are some matters on which the Church should stand against the tide of culture.

One major example of identity politics beginning to shape church culture is on the issue of gay rights. As we saw in Chapter

3, several major UK church bodies have already voted to bless gay marriages including the Methodist Church and the Church of Wales.

In 2020, the Church of England published its nearly 500-page report: *Living in Love and Faith*. The report was commissioned and led by the Bishops of the Church of England, and according to its blurb: 'A survey of what is happening in the world with regard to identity, sexuality, relationships and marriage is followed by an exploration of how Christians are to understand and respond to these trends in the light of the good news of Jesus Christ.'[10] However, the report does not put forward a set of doctrines or principles that summarise the Church of England's position on sex, gender and relationships. Rather, in quite a postmodern way, it simply lays out the various views within the denomination with fairly equal weighting and avoids drawing many firm conclusions. The report is freely open about this, saying in its introduction: 'this book offers no recommendations or guarantees of an agreed way forward for the church in relation to human identity, sexuality, relationships and marriage.'[10] For example, here is an excerpt from the report which discusses the diversity of sexualities and genders:

> One of the characteristic forms that sin takes is our failure to receive the God-given diversity of creation and of humanity as a gift... Many argue that this is exactly what has happened in the areas of gender and sexuality: that those who are not heterosexual, or who are not cisgender, are being treated as inferior- and that in the process something of the God-given richness and beauty of creation is being denied. On the other hand, many have wanted to insist that some of the differences that we find in human lives are not matters to celebrate, but are in some sense fractures or distortions.[10]

This paragraph presents opposing views on sexuality and gender side-by-side and makes little attempt to conclude which position is more faithful to the Bible's teaching.

In addition, *Living in Love and Faith* is laced throughout with vocabulary that seems to have been lifted straight out of the social justice campaigns. The report repeatedly speaks of the need for the Church of England to be 'more inclusive,' to 'stand against homophobia [and] transphobia,' and to value people's 'lived experience.'[10]

This is not the place for a detailed analysis of *Living in Love and Faith*. However, the relevant point is that we cannot ignore identity politics because, as *Living in Love and Faith* shows, identity politics is beginning to shape church culture and influence the highest levels of UK church leadership. 'Keep calm and carry on' is not an option anymore.

3. We Should Not Be Ashamed

We cannot ignore the identity politics revolution because it is now impacting both how our evangelistic messages are being received and how our churches are being shaped. But third and finally, we should engage with, and not ignore, identity politics because we ought not to be ashamed of the gospel.

In Romans 1:14-16, Paul explains to the church in Rome the reason for his ministry to them:

> I am obligated both to Greeks and non-Greeks, both to the wise and the foolish. That is why I am so eager to preach the gospel also to you who are in Rome. For I am not ashamed of the gospel, because it is the power of God that brings salvation to everyone who believes: first to the Jew, then to the Gentile.

Paul says that he is duty-bound to preach the gospel to everyone, because it is through hearing and believing the gospel that sinners can be saved. Paul clearly believes that the gospel is the greatest and most important message that anyone can hear and therefore he can proclaim: 'I am not ashamed of the gospel.' I find Paul's example convicting and challenging. The dangers Paul faced for preaching the gospel were far greater than being abused on Twitter or de-platformed at universities. By the time he wrote 2 Corinthians around AD 56, Paul could say:

> Five times I received from the Jews the forty lashes minus one. Three times I was beaten with rods, once I was pelted with stones, three times I was shipwrecked, I spent a night and a day in the open sea, I have been constantly on the move. I have been in danger from rivers, in danger from bandits, in danger from my fellow Jews, in danger from Gentiles; in danger in the city, in danger in the country, in danger at sea; and in danger from false believers. (2 Cor. 11:24-26)

There are many reasons to be careful, cautious, wise and even sometimes apprehensive about preaching the gospel and defending biblical truths in a world of identity politics. But one thing we should not be is ashamed. When we fear the societal repercussions of speaking for Jesus and when we are tempted to be ashamed of the gospel, we ought to remind ourselves and each other that the gospel is nothing short of 'the power of God that brings salvation to everyone who believes.' (Rom. 1:16)

Conclusion

I think the most common Christian response to identity politics is to simply ignore it. Whether it be out of fear, confusion, ignorance or simply having other priorities, many Christians have tried to ignore the revolution happening in our culture. However, evangelistic sermons that could once pack out stadiums are now viewed with suspicion; that is, if they get given a platform at all. Furthermore, we are now seeing identity politics beginning to shape and change the culture, policies and leadership of the Church. We surely cannot keep on going with business-as-usual and ignore the radical changes that are happening both in our society and in our churches. Christians need some sort of response to the ideas and ideologies of identity politics. The question is: what should that response be?

Part 3:
Finding a Way Through

9. The Power of the Narrative

'No matter how refined an algorithm or formula is, it can never match the flexible personal wisdom embedded in stories'
Annette Simmons, Whoever Tells the Best Story Wins

'Then Jesus told them this parable...'
Luke 15:3

In Part 1 of this book we explored the stories of the identity politics revolution, centring on the rise of feminism, the fight for racial justice, the story of gay pride, and the campaigns for trans rights. We then pulled the threads together to show that these diverse movements are united by an overarching narrative of the oppressed groups rising up to fight against and overthrow their societal oppressors. However, in this grand narrative, Christians have found themselves labelled as the oppressors: the bigoted, phobic, anti-progressive villains who need to be overthrown.

In Part 2, we saw three common Christian responses to identity politics. Many faithful Christians have sought to respond to the identity politics narrative by mirroring the campaigns of the activists, arguing the issues raised, or simply ignoring the whole thing entirely. However, as the last three chapters have unpacked, all three of these responses appear to be proving ineffectual at best and destructive at worst. So is there another way? Is there a better approach to speaking for Jesus in a world of identity politics?

This third and final Part attempts to sketch out the beginnings of an answer. Over the next two chapters, we will look at the power of storytelling and ask if Christians can tell a more powerful counter-narrative to that of identity politics. In Chapter 11 we will further explore the message of the cross and suggest that the gospel may resonate with our culture when Christians speak the language of the culture. Finally in Chapter 12, we will discuss how our actions should reflect our words, and how Christians should live practically and distinctively in a world of identity politics.

The Power of Storytelling

In 2009, journalist Rob Walker and author Josh Glenn set up a project in which they scoured charity shops and garage sales looking for cheap and random objects that they could sell on the shopping website eBay. However, before they sold their cheap objects on, Walker and Glenn gathered a group of around 100 authors who were each paired with an object and tasked with writing a fictional background story for their object. The objects were then posted on eBay, along with their fictional stories and a short biography of the author. The results were remarkable. The total initial cost of all the objects was $128.74, but when the stories were added, they sold of a total of $3,612.52! Among these was a painted bust of a horse's head which Walker and Glenn bought for 99 cents and sold on eBay for $62.95.[1] Walker and Glenn's project is an impressive (and lucrative) demonstration of the power of storytelling. Stories can capture hearts, subvert presuppositions, change behaviours and even make people part with their cash.

The power of storytelling to shape lives and influence ideas is becoming increasingly recognised, particularly in the world of business. In her aptly titled book *Whoever Tells the Best Story Wins*, President of Group Process Consulting Annette Simmons advises business leaders and entrepreneurs:

> Aristotle noted that craftsmen don't measure curves and indentations with a straightedge. Rather, they use a tape measure that bends and molds to forms. No matter how refined an algorithm or formula is, it can never match the flexible personal wisdom embedded in stories that can bend and mold, innovate and improvise.[2]

According to Simmons, if business leaders want to influence people's decisions, they should not reach for data, facts and rules as their primary tools, but rather for stories and narratives.

One of the sectors that has most effectively mastered the power of storytelling is, of course, the entertainment industry. In 2019 I went to see the Marvel film 'Avengers: Endgame' at a sold-out cinema on its opening weekend. (Warning: plot spoiler coming.) Following the cliff-hanger ending of its prequel 'Avengers: Infinity War,' which left half of all life in the universe dead, 'Endgame' was one of the most anticipated films of the year and became the highest-grossing film of all time. At a pivotal moment in the film, Iron Man, Thor and Captain America appear to lie defeated at the hands of their nemesis Thanos. But when all seems lost, suddenly Thor's hammer Mjølnir rises into the air and flies into the hand of Captain America – the first time in the entire Marvel movie saga that any character other than Thor had been deemed 'worthy' to wield the great weapon. At this moment in the film, something bizarre happened that I have never experienced in a cinema before or since – the audience erupted into spontaneous applause. Naturally, I could not help but join in. But who or what were we applauding? This was not a live theatre show; the actors and musicians could not hear us. So why applaud?

But of course it did not matter that the performers could not hear us, because we were applauding the *story*. The audience had become so invested in the fates of the characters that when we saw the first glimpse of our heroes clutching victory from the jaws of defeat, our excitement and joy overflowed into applause at a cinema screen. We had truly been captured by the power of storytelling.

One of the key reasons why stories are so powerful was delineated by political scientist Joseph Nye in his 1990 book *Bound to Lead*. Through this book Nye popularised the terms 'hard power' and 'soft power.'[3] According to Nye, hard power is deployed when leaders and governments try to make their people do things out of *compulsion* – through coercion and the wielding of authority. Conversely, soft power is deployed when leaders make people do things out of *attraction*, by influencing their desires and motivations. Hard power makes people do things; soft power makes people *want* to do things.

Storytelling wields soft power. It does not try to back opponents into an intellectual corner and compel them to change opinion. Rather it acknowledges the draw and beauty of the other competing voices, but then attracts people towards an even more captivating narrative.

The Stories of the Revolution

As we saw in the first Part of this book, the identity politics revolution has been largely driven not by scientific discoveries, or novel philosophies, or even political arguments. Rather, identity politics is predominantly driven by stories – both the personal stories of individuals finding identity, freedom and justice, and the grand overarching story of the oppressed rising up to fight against their societal oppressors.

America was captivated by the story of the young gay people in the Stonewall Inn who fought back against the police raid in 1969 and birthed the gay pride movement. Millions tuned in to hear the story of how Olympic hero Caitlyn Jenner had come to bravely and publicly self-identify as female. The tragic story of how George Zimmerman fatally shot the black seventeen-year-old Trayvon Martin, and was then acquitted of murder, produced furious backlash across the world as well as the founding of the Black Lives Matter organisation. And the appalling stories of sexual abuse perpetrated by Harvey Weinstein and other men in power sparked the global #MeToo movement, which empowered millions more women to share their stories of sexual harassment and assault.

In 2017, Emeritus Professor of Psychiatry Glynn Harrison published his popular book *A Better Story*. In *A Better Story*, Harrison explores why the sexual revolution swept through the Western world with such comprehensive impact in the 1970s and 80s. He argues that the power of the sexual revolution lay in its ability to tell captivating and powerful stories of people finding sexual liberty, freedom and joy through no-strings-attached sex. Harrison writes:

> Stories have the ability to grab people's attention, connect with their emotions, and open them up to the possibility of change. The change-makers of the sexual revolution understood this. They condensed complex intellectual arguments into memorable bite-size messages, and then wove them together into great stories... Much of the success of the sexual revolution can be attributed to its use of the entertainment industry as its main weapon of cultural subversion. But real-life stories of costly resistance and selfless compassion had a powerful impact in kindling people's individualistic moral reactions as well.[4]

For example, Harrison describes a short silent video that made the rounds on social media around the time leading up to the legalisation of gay marriage in the UK, titled 'Homecoming.'[4] The video depicts a group of British soldiers returning home from Afghanistan. As the military heroes disembark from the plane, they are applauded, greeted and hugged by their awaiting wives, girlfriends and children. But there is one male soldier who is left anxiously searching the crowd, until he spots a young man. They run towards each other in slow-motion, embrace, and then the soldier pulls out an engagement ring and gets down on one knee. The video closes with the on-screen text: 'All men can be heroes. All men can be husbands. End marriage discrimination.'

In just 100 seconds of video, the hearts of thousands of viewers were won – without any arguments, rhetoric or even spoken words. The video is another striking demonstration of the power of storytelling.

A Better Story

Herein lies the opportunity for evangelism. As we have seen in the last three chapters, the strategies of mirroring, arguing and ignoring our way through identity politics are proving ineffectual against the prevailing cultural narratives. Facts, arguments and condemnations seem only to strengthen the stories of freedom from oppression that paint Christians as the bigoted villains. But one thing Christians can do is tell stories. You cannot argue against a story, but you can out-narrate it with a better one. Therefore, perhaps Christians ought to be trying to answer the stories of the identity politics revolution with a more powerful counter-narrative: what Glynn Harrison calls 'a better story.' Here is how Harrison puts it:

> …we cannot engage with a great narrative by deploying more facts. We have to tell a different story. A better story. We must out-narrate those with whom we disagree. We shouldn't use narrative as a cynical debating device to

outwit our opponents and win the argument. We need to tell stories because this is how the human mind works, and because Jesus himself paved the way with some of the greatest stories ever told.[4]

Sam Chan takes these principles and applies them more broadly to evangelism in our postmodern world:

> We should use more stories in our evangelism. In modernity, people preferred hearing propositional data: "Give me the facts!" But in postmodernity, people prefer hearing stories: "Show me what this looks like." But stories also work well because they invite the hearer to see the world through our eyes... The hearer has to suspend their disbelief and enter my world...[5]

We live in a society where both sermonic preaching and apologetics debate are being increasingly and systematically cancelled by the culture. Therefore, when speaking for Jesus in a world of identity politics, perhaps we need a new kind of apologetics; we need to tell a better story.

Of course these ideas are not new. As Harrison mentions in the quote above, Christians follow and worship one of the greatest storytellers who has ever lived. In the gospel of Luke, Jesus tells a total of twenty-four parables; this is in a book with just twenty-four chapters! Jesus tells stories about: kings and servants, Pharisees and tax collectors, parents and children, builders and farmers, trees and fruit, coins and sheep. Jesus knew how to captivate listeners' hearts and minds with gospel stories.

So if we want to speak for Jesus effectively in this thorny and challenging world of identity politics, we can begin by asking: can we tell a better story?

A Familiar Story

So how can we tell a better story that engages the minds and hearts of those inspired and galvanised by the identity politics movements?

This may not be as difficult as it first appears. If we dig beneath the campaigns and activism of identity politics culture, and draw out the underlying principles and ideas that drive the movements, we quickly uncover a range of ideas that are actually profoundly biblical. Here are some of the terms that permeate identity politics discourse: freedom, liberation, justice, identity, diversity, equality, unity and peace. The Bible is saturated with these concepts. These should be Christian home-turf issues.

In a way, this should not surprise us. As we suggested in Chapter 5, one of the key reasons why identity politics has risen to dominance is because Western society has tried to abandon its historic Christian roots and is now attempting to fill the God-shaped void left behind. It would appear that identity politics does not just share its values with Christianity; it obtained its values *from* Christianity.

In the closing chapter of his book *Dominion*, historian Tom Holland argues that the whole of modern Western society, including the identity politics movements, has profoundly Christian historical foundations. He notes, for example, that those who campaign for abortion rights hold to the fundamentally Christian idea that a woman's body is her own and therefore ought to be respected by all men.[6] Furthermore, those who support gay marriage are strongly influenced by the Christian belief in the sanctity of monogamous matrimony.[6] And those who campaign for trans-inclusivity are driven by kindness and tolerance that is ultimately rooted in the Bible's teaching to 'love thy neighbour.'[6] The campaigns and goals of the social justice movements may have deviated significantly from the Bible's teaching in lots of ways. But many of the underlying principles that drive the movements can be traced back to the historical Christian roots of modern Western society. As Holland concludes:

> The trace elements of Christianity continued to infuse people's morals and presumptions so utterly that many failed even to detect their presence. Like dust particles so fine as to be invisible to the naked eye, they were breathed in equally by everyone: believers, atheists, and those who never paused so much as to think about religion. Had it been otherwise, then no one would ever have got woke.[6]

Here we have the foundations of a potential better story Christians can share with our culture. We can take these principles and ideas that drive the identity politics movement, such as liberty, justice and equality, and use them to show how the gospel is the true, ultimate and better story.

What would this better story actually look like? That is what the next chapter will be all about.

Conclusion

The rise of identity politics calls for a rethink in the way we approach evangelism. In today's society, zealous preachers are often ignored as antiquated voices from a patriarchal age, and astute apologists are cancelled as dissenting voices that oppose progress and liberty. However, one thing Christians can do is tell stories. Stories have immense power to captivate hearts, change lives and subvert arguments. Many of the campaigns of identity politics have been propelled by powerful stories of equality, liberty, identity and justice – ideas that have deep roots in biblical Christianity. Herein lies the opportunity: to acknowledge the power and principles of the identity politics movements, but then to tell the Bible's Bigger, better and more complete story.

What would that better story look like? In the next chapter, we begin to sketch out an answer.

10. Have You Heard The One About…?

'I will sing the wondrous story,
Of the Christ who died for me'
Francis Rowley, I Will Sing the Wondrous Story (hymn)

In the last chapter, we explored the power of storytelling to captivate minds and change lives. We also saw that the identity politics revolution has been driven by powerful stories and narratives, many of which are actually rooted in deeply biblical principles. In light of this, we suggested that Christians ought to respond to our culture not with facts, rule and condemnations, but by setting out to tell a better story.

In this chapter, we will attempt to do just that. In each section of this chapter, we will take one key principle that drives a significant part of identity politics culture. We will explore how the social justice movements value and uphold this principle but also how they tell an incomplete or imperfect story in some way. We will then try to show how the Bible provides a more complete and fulfilling story.

These stories are far from comprehensive. But I hope that the following short sections may become seedlings to whet appetites and spark imaginations as we collectively consider how to bring the gospel to our culture.

Equality

One tenet at the heart of all the social justice movements is equality – the principle that everyone should be considered as having the same worth, regardless of their skin-colour, sexuality, gender or any other attribute. In the UK, the 2010 Equality Act enshrines the equality of all citizens into law and prohibits discrimination on grounds of a number of 'protected characteristics.' The founding fathers of the US not only wrote equality into the US Declaration of Independence, but also pronounced it 'self-evident.'[1]

Yet despite equality being enshrined in law, modern society is still permeated with inequality. The often-quoted gender pay gap and the under-representation of women in executive positions appear to show that society still does not treat men and women equally. The disproportionately high numbers of fatal police shootings of black people,[2] such as Trayvon Martin and Michael Brown, appear to demonstrate institutionalised prejudice and racial discrimination in the police, which can have deadly consequences. And so, the social justice movements are fighting to uncover and deconstruct the systems of inequality and discrimination that exist across our society.

But does identity politics really give the best and most fulfilling answer to inequality? Or might it be an incomplete story?

For example, positive discrimination has undoubtably helped to redress some institutional inequalities, such as helping the UK parliament become more demographically representative of the country's electorate, at least in terms of gender. But it has also angered some minority groups such as the Asian students who sued Harvard University over their 'race conscious' admission policy which appeared to discriminate against Asian students.[3]

Or to take another example, academic courses such as Whiteness Studies and Critical Race Theory have drawn awareness to the societal and institutional structures that ostensibly disadvantage and discriminate against ethnic minorities. But when Whiteness Studies teaches that all white people are privileged and implicated in racism, does this really empower ethnic minorities? Or might it simply sharpen racial divisions?

And there is also a more fundamental question that is worth asking: where do we get this idea of equality from? Or to put it another way: why should we consider all people equal?

For the majority of recorded human history, the equality of all people was not a universally-held belief and it was certainly not seen as 'self-evident.' For example, in the Ancient Graeco-Roman world, society was built on the presupposition that not all people were equal. The Greek philosopher Aristotle put it this way, in his book *Politics*:

> ...is not all slavery a violation of nature? There is no difficulty in answering this question, on grounds both of reason and of fact. For that some should rule and others be ruled is a thing not only necessary, but expedient; from the hour of their birth, some are marked out for subjection, others for rule.[4]

Aristotle taught, and the Ancient Graeco-Roman world lived out, a belief that not everyone is equal, but rather that those born strong and competitive are destined for success and rule, whilst those born weak and inferior are destined for subjugation. The Ancient world did not widely view all people as intrinsically equal.

But perhaps more disconcertingly, the worldview of materialism, that views the universe as being composed of nothing more than matter and energy, naturally leads to a similar conclusion. In his best-selling book *Sapiens*, philosopher Yuval Noah Harari writes: 'According to the science of biology, people were not "created." They have evolved. And they certainly did not evolve to be "equal." Evolution is based on difference, not on equality.'[5] If Harari is right that humans are nothing more than organic machines that have evolved to propagate our DNA, then evolution dictates that the strong should survive and the weak should die out. Therefore, it is difficult to find an objective biological reason to view all people as equally valuable. Equality cannot be derived from biology.

How then have we ended up in a society that widely assumes the intrinsic equality of all people? What happened between Aristotle and today that so radically transformed the world's views on equality?

The historical answer seems clear. One of the primary reasons why the value of equality became increasingly popular and accepted throughout the Ancient world was because of the rise of Christianity.

In Genesis 1:27 we read: 'So God created mankind in his own image, in the image of God he created them; male and female he created them.' In making human beings in His image, God endowed each person with intrinsic, immutable, immense and *equal* value, independent of our skin colour, sexuality, age, gender, abilities, productivity, or how much society values us. We do not need to create value for ourselves or earn value from others. Rather, we are given intrinsic value through our creation as image-bearers of God. This gives human beings radical equality, as Emeritus Professor of Ethics and Perinatology John Wyatt writes in his book *Matters of Life and Death*:

> We are all equal because we all bear the family likeness. The need for justice, equality and fairness in human society comes from our radical equality by creation... In the human community, we are surrounded by other reflections of God who are different but fundamentally equal in dignity to ourselves.[6]

When we get to the book of Leviticus, we see God commanding the Israelites: 'When a foreigner resides among you in your land, do not mistreat them. The foreigner residing among you must be treated as your native-born. Love them as yourself, for you were foreigners in Egypt' (Lev. 19:33-34). Here we have the equality between races enshrined in Mosaic Law; the Israelites were to treat foreigners residing amongst them as legally equal to themselves.

Then in the New Testament, we see Jesus, the King of heaven and earth, being born in the squalor of an animal feeding trough, and then growing up to associate with the most disregarded and devalued people in His society. Jesus demonstrated by His words and actions that He valued the lives of the people the Ancient world looked down on, including children, widows, lepers, prostitutes and the disabled.

Because God has created all people with intrinsic and equal value, Christians are also called to treat all people with equal dignity and respect, regardless of their physical, mental or social attributes. In James 1:27-2:4, James writes:

> Religion that God our Father accepts as pure and faultless is this: to look after orphans and widows in their distress and to keep oneself from being polluted by the world. My brothers and sisters, believers in our glorious Lord Jesus Christ must not show favouritism. Suppose a man comes into your meeting wearing a gold ring and fine clothes, and a poor man in filthy old clothes also comes in. If you show special attention to the man wearing fine clothes and say, "Here's a good seat for you," but say to the poor man, "You stand there" or "Sit on the floor by my feet," have you not discriminated among yourselves and become judges with evil thoughts?

James overturns the social hierarchy of the culture. He commands his readers to emulate Jesus by caring for the vulnerable in society and treating the rich and poor with equality.

As Tom Holland points out, it was these biblical teachings on the equality of all people that led the Medieval Christian cannon lawyers in the twelfth and thirteenth centuries to coin the concept of 'universal human rights.' As Holland writes:

> The evolution of the concept of human rights mediated as it had been since the Reformation by Protestant jurists and philosophes, had come to obscure its original authors. It derived, not from ancient Greece or Rome... It is an inheritance from the [Christian] canon lawyers of the Middle Ages.[7]

Human Rights were not invented by Greek philosophers, or naturalistic Enlightenment thinkers, or social justice activists. They were invented by Christian canon lawyers who believed that all people are equally entitled to Human Rights because all people are equally made in God's image.

The social justice movements are surely right in their endeavour to fight for equality for all people. However, underneath their drive for equality is a philosophical vacuum. If humans are nothing more than atoms, molecules and DNA, then there is little reason to treat everyone as equal or to value and protect those who are evolutionarily disadvantaged. But if there is a God, who made all people in His image, and who commands His followers to value the disregarded and disadvantaged, then we have a profound and powerful reason to fight for equality.

The Evil of Oppression

Another key idea that underpins the identity politics narrative is the evil of oppression. Identity politics tells the story of the oppressed minority groups waking up to their oppression, and then rising up to fight against their societal oppressors.

The #MeToo movement that began in 2017 has brought down hundreds of men with power and influence who have used their positions to oppress, harass and abuse women. The recent church abuse revelations have shone a light on oppressive cultures within churches, where church leaders have used their spiritual and institutional power to abuse people who were meant to be under their spiritual care. Across society there are far too many people in power who feel entitled to abuse their authority and oppress those less powerful than themselves.

Furthermore, as a range of psychological studies have shown, this tendency to oppress can sometimes be unconscious.[8] Individuals may not even be aware of their own prejudices and discriminatory biases that lead them to complicity in oppression. Therefore, there is now a drive to roll out unconscious bias training programmes and courses across public and private sector institutions, so that the biases that lead to complicity in oppression can be uncovered and addressed.

However, does identity politics really give the best and most satisfying answer to the evil of oppression?

Unconscious bias training has helped to raise awareness of the internalised prejudices that people may not even be aware that they harbour. But should we be rolling out unconscious bias training across society, when there is currently little evidence that it changes behaviour?[9] Or to take another example, banning and de-platforming speakers who incite violence and hatred has proven to be an important way of protecting vulnerable people from harassment and danger. But does cancelling speakers like Germaine Greer and Franklin Graham really help combat oppression, or does it simply suppress debate and censor those who hold opinions that activists disagree with?

But more fundamentally, is the framing of society as 'oppressor versus oppressed' really an accurate and adequate anthropology? Identity politics splits the population down demographic lines and labels one side 'oppressed' and the other side 'oppressor.' As a result, we have books such as *White Fragility* by Robin DiAngelo which argue that all white people are complicit in racism and racial oppression simply by virtue of them being white. But can we really bisect society into good and bad? If we honestly reflect on our own hearts, desires and motivations, do we not all encounter a complex mixture of both good and bad within us?

In 1973, the Russian novelist and Soviet dissident Aleksandr Solzhenitsyn published *The Gulag Archipelago* – an account based on his experiences as a prisoner in the Soviet Gulags. As he reflects on the oppression, forced labour and cruelty he experienced and witnessed in the Gulags, Solzhenitsyn concludes, perhaps surprisingly, not that some people are wholly evil whilst others are wholly good. Rather, he writes: 'The line separating good and evil passes not through states, nor between classes, nor between political parties either – but right through every human heart.'[10] Each one of us has both good and evil running through our core.

This is where Christian faith can provide a more profound and satisfying diagnosis of human nature than identity politics.

The Bible teaches that all evil, oppression, divisiveness and abuse stems from the reality of sin. In Genesis 3 we read that through Adam and Eve's rebellion against God's commands, sin entered the world. As a result, their relationships with God, each other and the rest of creation were fractured. Then, as Genesis 3 continues, we see the introduction of rivalry and animosity into the world, as Adam blames Eve for giving him the fruit to eat (Gen. 3:12). We also see subjugation come into the world as God curses Eve saying: 'Your desire will be for your husband, and he will rule over you' (Gen. 3:16b). Oppression within relationships is a curse, not a command. Then, in Genesis 4 we read of jealously, pride, vengeance and murder within the first family tree; sin had become inherent to the human race. This is what Augustine of Hippo termed 'Original Sin'- the doctrine that all humans, Jesus notwithstanding, are born into an inherently sinful nature. As Rico Tice and Barry Cooper write in the *Christianity Explored* book:

> If we were to trace all the evil in the world, back to its source, the place we'd end up is the human heart... Why is it so hard to keep good relationships going? Why do we hurt even those we love most? Why aren't people at

work more co-operative? Because each of us has a heart problem.[11]

But sin does not just lead to relationship breakdown. It also leads to spiritual blindness. As Paul writes: 'They are darkened in their understanding and separated from the life of God because of the ignorance that is in them due to the hardening of their hearts' (Eph. 4:18). Jesus makes a similar point in John 9 when he heals a man who had been blind since birth. Jesus explains: 'For judgment I have come into this world, so that the blind will see and those who see will become blind' (John 9:39). Some self-righteous Pharisees then ask Him: 'What? Are we blind too?' (John 9:40), to which Jesus responds: 'If you were blind, you would not be guilty of sin; but now that you claim you can see, your guilt remains' (John 9:41). This is sometimes called the 'noetic effects of sin'; sin corrupts our minds and spiritually blinds us, including to the reality of our own sinfulness and our need for salvation. Our sin is responsible both for the evil in our hearts and for our blindness to this evil.

So as we observe and become outraged by acts of oppression and abuse in our society, and as we uncover the unconscious biases that we individually harbour, maybe these are pointing us towards a deeper reality about our humanity. Perhaps the world is filled with oppression and unconscious biases because the human heart is both corrupted and blinded by sin, which ultimately makes us want to be gods of our lives, even if that involves harming and oppressing those less powerful than ourselves.

If this is true, then the solution to oppression must go much further than simply dichotomising society into good and bad. As we shall see in the next few sections, what we need is a universal, comprehensive and eternal solution to the problem of sin.

Liberty

The narrative of identity politics does not just frame society as a struggle between the oppressed and the oppressors. It also implores the oppressed to fight for their liberation.

This desire for freedom and liberation from oppressive structures has driven many of the social justice campaigns and policies, from the legalisation of gay marriage, to the permitting of trans people to self-identify as their gender identity. When the Court of Appeal ruled that clinicians are permitted to prescribe puberty blockers to transgender children[12] (overturning the previous High Court decision which prohibited their use),[13] the trans children's charity Mermaids responded: 'This is a victory for... young people's bodily autonomy.'[14] At the heart of these campaigns is the principle that all people should be free to live as they please, in a diverse and tolerant society. Furthermore, institutions such as the Church, which set rules and edicts that appear to restrict people's liberties, are seen as the oppressive villains who need to be overthrown.

However, does identity politics really give the best and most complete story of liberty and freedom?

After all, not all of the policies of the social justice activists, that claim to increase liberty, have been uncontroversial. For example, allowing children to explore their beliefs, rather than imposing ideas on them, is an essential part of educating children to think freely for themselves. But is teaching children to minimise the significance of their biological sex, or even raising them in a gender-neutral environment such as Egalia Pre-School in Stockholm,[15] really the best and most liberating pedagogy, particularly for children who do not conform to culturally sanctioned gender stereotypes? As gay rights activist Kate Harris argues,[16] may this approach to education actually reinforce unhelpful and restrictive stereotypes, as girls perceived as 'masculine' and boys perceived as 'feminine' are no longer accepted for their idiosyncrasies but instead pressured to transition?

Another contentious area for the social justice movements is freedom of conscience. Anti-discrimination laws are crucial to ensure that everyone can freely live and access all parts of society independent of their race, gender or sexuality. But might compelling opponents to either openly support the social justice movements, or risk censorship, undermine the human right to conscience? When Gareth Lee sued Ashers Bakery for refusing to write a pro-gay-marriage slogan on a personalised cake, he alleged that he had been the victim of unlawful discrimination.[17] But, as the Supreme Court upheld, there is a key difference between protecting individuals from personal discrimination, and compelling people to say or print statements of beliefs that they disagree with.[18] Would eroding people's rights to live, act and speak in line with their consciences really lead to a more liberal and free society?

However, all of these issues are underpinned by an even more fundamental question: what does it mean to be free? Identity politics is built on the assumption that freedom comes when individuals are given total autonomy in how they live their lives. Therefore, any rules, institutions or people who restrict this autonomy are labelled as anti-liberal and oppressive. But is this really freedom? After all, if we lived in a society where everyone always acted the way they wanted without any rule or regulation, it would be anarchy not paradise. Furthermore, in everyday life we all regularly let go of our autonomy, in order to gain greater freedom and flourishing in the long term. Each time we hand our car keys over to the mechanic, or self-isolate when we catch an infectious disease, or send our children to school, we forego our autonomy in the hope of reaping longer-term benefits.

Herein lies the opportunity for Christians to tell a better story about liberation.

In Exodus 1, we see God's people become enslaved by the tyrannical Pharoah of Egypt and forced to do ruthless manual labour on Pharoah's building sites. But after God sends ten plagues that devastate the nation of Egypt, including the death of every firstborn at Passover (Ex. 11-12), the Israelites are finally freed and leave Egypt to journey to the Promised Land. God commands the Israelites to continually remember the Passover as their great national redemption story. Even before the Passover has actually happened, whilst they are still in Egypt, Moses institutes the Passover remembrance ceremony, saying to the elders of Israel: 'Obey these instructions as a lasting ordinance for you and your descendants. When you enter the land that the LORD will give you as he promised, observe this ceremony' (Ex. 12:24-25).

When we get to the New Testament, it becomes clear that the Passover was a foreshadowing of the great and ultimate rescue mission of the cross. The gospel writers repeatedly point out that Jesus' crucifixion happened during the Passover period, and in 1 Corinthians 5:7, Paul calls Jesus 'our Passover lamb.' The cross is framed as the ultimate story of rescue from the slavery of sin and death, so that through Jesus, we may experience true freedom in Him. As Jesus Himself declares: 'So if the Son sets you free, you will be free indeed' (John 8:36).

So, to return to the question we previously posed: what does it mean to be free?

In Romans 6, Paul describes our slavery to sin from which we need rescuing: 'When you were slaves to sin, you were free from the control of righteousness. What benefit did you reap at that time from the things you are now ashamed of? Those things result in death!' (Rom. 6:20-21). Sin enslaves us from the inside, preventing us from living righteously and condemning us to lives destined for the grave.

But then Paul goes on to describe the freedom found in Jesus: 'But now that you have been set free from sin and have become slaves of God, the benefit you reap leads to holiness, and the result is eternal life. For the wages of sin is death, but the gift of God is eternal life in Christ Jesus our Lord' (Rom. 6:22-23).

According to Paul, true freedom is not found in absolute autonomy. Rather, freedom is found in *holiness*. If sin is living in opposition to God and His moral laws, then holiness is living in line with God's created moral order. Therefore, true and ultimate freedom can only be found through realigning our lives back to our Creator's intended moral framework.

Paul makes a similar point in Galatians 5 when he writes: 'It is for freedom that Christ has set us free...You, my brothers and sisters, were called to be free. But do not use your freedom to indulge the flesh; rather, serve one another humbly in love. For the entire law is fulfilled in keeping this one command: "Love your neighbour as yourself"' (Gal. 5:1, 13-14).

Christian freedom can perhaps be compared to a camera lens that can only capture a sharp photo when dialled to the correct mode, or a car that can only drive when it is filled with the correct fuel. The photographer is free to capture whatever they like with the camera, and the driver is free to travel wherever they like in the car, providing that these objects are used in the way they were designed to be used. To do otherwise would be restrictive, not liberating. As Glynn Harrison puts it: 'We flourish as human beings when we work with, rather than against, the grain of God's reality.'[19]

Therefore, when we read the Bible's commands, we should not see a set of repressive diktats that we begrudgingly follow out of guilt or fear. Rather we should see the Creator's solid moral framework on which we can build the free and flourishing lives we all desire and God intends.

To take one pertinent example, the commands to maintain sex within the boundaries of lifelong and biblically-defined matrimony are not given to restrict our freedom or repress our sexual identity. Rather, they are provided as the framework and context in which we can experience the kind of true, pure and intimate sexual freedom that our Creator intended.

That is not to say that obeying Christ is easy or comfortable – it often is not. But it is profoundly liberating.

One of the best storytellers of this freedom found in Jesus was the Methodist hymn writer Charles Wesley. In his famous hymn 'And Can It Be?' Wesley writes:

> Long my imprisoned spirit lay,
> Fast bound in sin and nature's night
> Thine eye diffused a quickening ray
> I woke, the dungeon flamed with light
> My chains fell off, my heart was free
> I rose, went forth, and followed Thee.

Identity

Another key plotline in the identity politics narrative is the quest for identity. We all want to write ourselves into a grand narrative that gives our lives meaning, significance and purpose. Therefore, some of the most important and meaningful things in life are to find our identity, to remain true to it, and for this identity to be recognised by others. And so, when identity groups experience oppression or discrimination from people, institutions and society at large, many respond by coalescing around their identity groups and rising up to fight for their rights and recognition.

The mantra of Stonewall, according to their website, is not simply to campaign for legal rights for gay people, but rather to 'imagine a world where all LGBTQ+ people are free to be ourselves.'[20] Here Stonewall frames gay rights less in terms of what gay people do, and more around who gay people *are*.

This narrative of identity is also central to the trans rights movement. In her 1992 pamphlet *Trans Gender Liberation,* Leslie Feinberg argued for the need to stand up for trans rights because no-one should be 'punished for their self-expression.'[21]

The Scottish Government's Supporting Transgender Pupils in Schools guidance states that when a teacher talks to a pupil who is exploring or questioning their gender, it is 'important not to deny their identity.'[22]

However, does identity politics really give the best and most complete answer to people's need for identity?

After all, some of the policies of the social justice activists, that are intended to protect and uphold the identities of minorities, have proven contentious. For example, the use of language such as 'chest-feeding'[23] or 'bodies with vaginas'[24] is intended to be inclusive of trans and non-binary identities. But these phrases have triggered backlash as some have argued that they demean the identities of women by reducing them to their body parts.

Furthermore, many trans activists contend that respecting trans people's identities necessarily involves allowing all trans people, including children, access to cross-sex hormones and transition surgery upon request. But is this really the best way to uphold all trans people's identities? Where does that leave people like Keira Bell or Walt Heyer who medically transitioned and then discovered that their dysphoria and identity struggles were not solved by transitioning?[25,26]

This is where Christianity can provide a much richer and better story of identity.

The Bible paints a beautiful and vivid image of the life-changing identity Christians receive from God, rooted in our creation, adoption and inheritance.

Firstly, the Bible speaks of our identity inherent in our creation. David writes in Psalm 8:5, 'You have made them [mankind] a little lower than the angels and crowned them with glory and honour.'

In our creation, God gives humans status. We may have been made from the dust of the earth (Gen. 2:7), but God endows us with a rank just below the great angelic hosts of heaven. Furthermore, He has crowned us; we are declared by God to be royalty. But perhaps most remarkably of all, God gives us glory. Four verses earlier, David has written that God has set His own glory in the Heavens (Ps. 8:1). But then in verse 5, God crowns *us* with glory and honour.

David then goes on in Psalm 8:6-8 to describe mankind's place on earth:

'You made them rulers over the works of your hands;

    you put everything under their feet:

all flocks and herds,

    and the animals of the wild,

the birds in the sky,

    and the fish in the sea,

    all that swim the paths of the seas.'

God creates mankind and gives us the job of ruling over creation as God's delegated leaders on earth. God values our identities so greatly that He entrusts us with the whole of His world. We are His royal and glorified rulers on earth.

So firstly, our identity is rooted in our creation. But secondly, it is rooted in our adoption as sons and daughters of God.

In Ephesians 1:4-6, Paul writes: 'In love he predestined us for adoption to sonship through Jesus Christ, in accordance with his pleasure and will- to the praise of his glorious grace, which he has freely given us in the One he loves.' As Christians we have been chosen by God since before the creation of the world to be adopted into His heavenly family. And the adoption fees were not cheap; they cost God the life of His begotten Son. I once heard the preacher Jonathan Lamb at the Keswick Convention tell the story of a child who was being bullied at school because he was adopted as a baby. The child became so exasperated by the bullies that one day he turned round and said to them: 'You can say what you like, but my parents chose me!'[27] God doesn't tolerate us reluctantly. He joyfully welcomes us as those He has freely chosen since before the creation of the world to be part of His family.

Christians find our identity in our creation as royal stewards of the earth and in our adoption as chosen children of God. Third and finally we find our identity in our inheritance as Christ's co-heirs.

In Romans 8:17, Paul writes: 'Now if we are children, then we are heirs– heirs of God and co-heirs with Christ, if indeed we share in his sufferings in order that we may also share in his glory.' Not only does our adoption give us a secure identity now, but it also gives us an inheritance to come, as we become co-heirs with Christ the King. When we get to the letter to the church in Laodicea in Revelation 3, we hear Jesus make the astonishing declaration: 'To the one who is victorious, I will give the right to sit with me on my throne, just as I was victorious and sat down with my Father on his throne' (Rev. 3:21). Christ's throne will one day become our throne, as we become the sanctified, glorified and eternal heirs of God.

In Christ we have a new, glorious and immutable identity, rooted in our creation, adoption and inheritance. This grand story, into which our lives can fit, gives us far more security, significance and self-worth than anything identity politics, or indeed the world at large, can offer.

In Galatians 3:28-29, Paul writes: 'There is neither Jew nor Gentile, neither slave nor free, nor is there male and female, for you are all one in Christ Jesus. If you belong to Christ, then you are Abraham's seed, and heirs according to the promise.' Although racial, occupational, gender, legal and societal identities are important and real, they are eclipsed by the Christian's new identity in Christ. Our identity in Christ is far bigger, more secure, more long-lasting and more satisfying than any other identity we could forge or find. This means that our other identities such as our gender, race or sexuality no longer need to bear the weight of our whole self-worth. We matter, not because of our appearance, attributes, attractions or achievements; we matter because of who Christ says we are.

As pastor Vaughan Roberts puts it in his book *Transgender*:

> We will always be insecure if our identity is based on something within us: our feelings, assertions or achievements. But this new identity in Christ that he offers us could not be more secure. We will often fail God, but our relationship with him remains unshakeable because it is founded not on anything we do but on what Christ has already done for us.[28]

Justice

The final principle that we are going to explore in this chapter is justice. Justice is a precious and integral cornerstone of modern society. Over recent decades, powerful public spotlights have been shone on a range of moral atrocities from the sexual abuse cases that sparked the #MeToo movement, to the killings of unarmed black people by US police officers, leading thousands round the world to demand justice for the victims. More broadly, the social justice movements aim to uncover systemic and institutional injustices that have oppressed and disadvantaged minority groups. The need for justice for the victims of wrongdoing is a conviction that runs deep through the human heart. When those in power oppress and abuse others, they must pay the penalty for their actions.

However, does identity politics really give the best and most fulfilling answer to the great injustices in the world?

Over recent years, the social justice movements have been instrumental in bringing some powerful individuals to justice for their crimes. Following the murder of George Floyd, massive protests around the world culminated in his murderer Derek Chauvin being sentenced to 22.5 years in prison. Protesters also expressed their anger at historic racial injustices by toppling the statues of controversial figures including MP and slave-trader Edward Colston in Bristol. These were powerful symbolic demonstrations of communities' commitment to root out racism and racial injustices. But what about justice for Colston's victims?

What can we do about the great injustice of the likes of Colston dying before they could be held accountable for their wrongdoings?

Looking more broadly at society, does identity politics really give the best answer to dealing with systemic and institutional injustices? It is one thing to reform society in a way that makes it more tolerant and equal. But does reporting homophobic or racist comments made by nursey children to Local Education Authorities on grounds of 'hate speech' really help to bring about justice for the oppressed?[29] Might this be a disproportionate and even unjust punishment on children making mistakes?

But there is also a much more fundamental question that is worth asking: where do we get this principle of justice from? Why should good actions be rewarded and bad actions be punished?

After all, in the worldview of materialism, morality and justice are little more than societal constructs. In his book *River Out of Eden*, Richard Dawkins writes: 'In a universe of electrons and selfish genes, blind physical forces and genetic replication, some people are going to get hurt, other people are going to get lucky, and you won't find any rhyme or reason in it, nor any justice.'[30]

According to Dawkins, if there is no God, and if the universe is nothing more than physical elements and processes, then morality and justice lose their metaphysical grounding. Our convictions, that morality needs to be upheld and justice needs to be served, are nothing more than evolved instincts and social conventions. There is no moral law book in the sky to hold people accountable to. As biologist Thomas Henry Huxley points out: 'evolution may teach us how the good and evil tendencies of man have come about but, in itself it is incomplete to furnish any... reason why what we call "good" is preferable to what we call "evil."'[31] If someone says something is right when we see it as wrong, on what authority can we impose our morality on them?

Some point out that incarcerating individuals such as Derek Chauvin and Harvey Weinstein is necessary to rehabilitate their immoral behaviour and protect potential further victims. This is of course true and important. However, the social justice movements are also driven by a deeper conviction that justice must be served. Black Lives Matter did not simply call for Derek Chauvin to changes his ways; they called for him to pay the penalty for his wrongdoings. But how can we hold people accountable for their actions when there is no objective moral standard to hold them to?

This is where Christians can provide a more solid foundation for our conviction that justice needs to be served.

The Bible teaches that there is an objective moral law because there is an objective moral lawgiver.

In Deuteronomy 32:3-4, Moses proclaims to the assembly of Israel:

'I will proclaim the name of the Lord.
    Oh, praise the greatness of our God!
He is the Rock, his works are perfect,
    and all his ways are just.
A faithful God who does no wrong,
    upright and just is he.'

God is the epitome and embodiment of all that is good and righteous.

But God is not a detached, passive moral observer of the world. Morality is not a hidden code that needs be cracked through philosophical introspection or intellectual innovation. Rather, God has revealed His moral goodness through His Word. As David writes in Psalm 19:7-8:

'The law of the Lord is perfect,
    refreshing the soul.
The statutes of the Lord are trustworthy,
    making wise the simple.
The precepts of the Lord are right,
    giving joy to the heart.
The commands of the Lord are radiant,
    giving light to the eyes.'

God is the embodiment of moral goodness, and so we can know what is good when we know God's commands.

Furthermore, because God is good, He cares about justice when His moral laws are broken. He cares deeply about how we treat each other and His world, and therefore He gets righteously angry when injustices are committed. As the psalmist writes of God in Psalm 89:14: 'Righteousness and justice are the foundation of your throne; love and faithfulness go before you.' In a world filled with so many leaders and powerful individuals who use their positions to further their own power and supremacy, is there not a real need for leadership founded in justice and righteousness?

Because God cares about injustices, He will one day come to judge the world and bring about true and complete justice on all those who have done wrong, including those who died before they could be held accountable for their actions on earth. As Paul writes in 2 Corinthians 5:10: 'For we must all appear before the judgment seat of Christ, so that each of us may receive what is due us for the things done while in the body, whether good or bad.' The judgment of God is good news, because it means that all those who oppress others or abuse their power will face the consequences of their actions, and their victims will see true, complete and final justice served.

However, the coming judgment of God does not mean Christians should sit idle as injustices are committed around us. Rather, the moral goodness of God should lead Christians to act justly. In Micah 6, God reminds the people of Israel of His goodness towards them, particularly in rescuing them from slavery in Egypt (Micah 6:4). Micah then tells the Israelites how they ought to respond:

'He has shown you, O mortal, what is good.
    And what does the LORD require of you?
To act justly and to love mercy
    and to walk humbly with your God.' (Micah 6:8)

The goodness of God should lead His people to manifest His justice and mercy in the world. Christians should fight against injustice because God cares for the sinned-against. In doing so, we prophetically point others to the justice of God, by upholding His justice in the world. (We will be exploring more about what this practically looks like in Chapter 12.)

The Bible's story of justice is far richer, more robust and more hopeful than anything our culture can offer. God gives us reason to believe in justice, hope that justice will be served on the final Day of Judgment, and motivation to fight for justice in our society.

Conclusion

In this chapter we have tried to sketch out some ways in which Christians can tell the Bible's better story to our culture. Identity politics is driven by principles such as equality, identity, liberty and justice, which have deep historic Christian roots. Therefore, Christians have an opportunity to show that although the stories offered by identity politics are attractive and galvanising, they are also incomplete and ultimately unsatisfying. Then we can go on to tell the Bible's bigger and better story.

The sections in this chapter are certainly not intended to be exhaustive or paradigmatic. Rather they are simply suggestions to spark imaginations and whet appetites as we consider how to reach our culture with the gospel.

In the next chapter will be diving even deeper into evangelism as we look at the language of the cross and its power to resonate with the cultures of the world. But we end this chapter echoing the encouraging words of Francis Rowley's hymn:

> I will sing the wondrous story, of the Christ who died for me.
> How He left His home in glory for the cross of Calvary.
> I was lost, but Jesus found me, found the sheep that went astray,
> Threw His loving arms around me, drew me back into His way.

11. Speaking the Language of the Culture

'I have become all things to all people so that by all possible means I might save some'
Apostle Paul, 1 Corinthians 9:22

'World evangelization requires the whole Church to take the whole gospel to the whole world'
The Lausanne Covenant

In 1 Corinthians 9:20-22, Paul writes to the Corinthian church:

> To the Jews I became like a Jew, to win the Jews. To those under the law I became like one under the law (though I myself am not under the law), so as to win those under the law. To those not having the law I became like one not having the law (though I am not free from God's law but am under Christ's law), so as to win those not having the law. To the weak I became weak, to win the weak. I have become all things to all people so that by all possible means I might save some.

Throughout the book of Acts, we see Paul doing exactly this: becoming all things to all people so that the gospel might gain a hearing. When he preaches to the Jews in the synagogue in Thessalonica, Paul expounds the Old Testament Scriptures and uses them to show that Jesus is the Messiah (Acts 17:1-4). When he debates with the Athenian philosophers and intellects at the Areopagus, Paul quotes Cretan and Cilician philosophers and demonstrates his knowledge of the religious culture of the city (Acts 17:16-34). When he is arrested and put on trial before King Agrippa, Paul does what is expected from defendants on trial and tells Agrippa his personal testimony – albeit an unusual one (Acts 26:1-32).

Of course, the core of Paul's message of salvation remained the same wherever he went. However, the ways Paul presented and framed the message changed depending on his context and audience.

In this chapter, we will be diving deeper into the message of the cross and how we can preach the cross whilst becoming 'all things to all people' in a world of identity politics. In order to do this, we will explore two books that I have found particularly helpful in thinking about evangelism in the modern world. These books are: *The 3D Gospel* by Jayson Georges and *The Cross of Christ* by John Stott.

The 3D Gospel

In his book *The 3D Gospel,* missiologist Jayson Georges explores the idea that world cultures can be broadly grouped into three main categories. Georges identifies these three cultural groups as:

1. 'Guilt-Innocence Cultures' – These are individualistic cultures, situated mostly in the global West. In guilt-innocence cultures, moral wrongdoing is usually framed in terms of legal rule-breaking and the consequences predominantly manifest in judicial retribution. Much of

the necessities for life, such as resources and information, are controlled by governments and institutions, and therefore access to these things is gained through obedience to their institutional stipulations.

2. 'Shame-Honour Cultures' – These are collectivistic cultures, predominantly found in the global East. In shame-honour cultures, immoral actions are primarily seen as bringing shame and dishonour on families and communities, and wrongs are rectified when community honour is restored. Resources and information are largely possessed not by institutions but by the community and therefore access to these necessities is obtained through maintaining relationships and reputation.

3. 'Fear-Power Cultures' – These are animistic contexts typically located in the global South. Fear-power cultures are more acutely aware of omens, spirits and supernatural realm, and therefore immorality is framed less in terms of rule-breaking, or community dishonour, but more in terms of provoking the spiritual realm. Therefore safety, security and good fortune in life are obtained through consulting, obeying and pleasing the spirit world, often through rituals, incantations or divinations.[1]

Georges then goes on to propose that the message of the gospel has powerfully impacted all three of these cultures. However, Georges observes that the gospel *presentation* that has resonated *most* differs between each of the cultures.

Georges suggests that in guilt-innocence cultures, the gospel message that has made the most profound impact begins with the idea that all human beings have broken the moral laws of our holy and righteous God (Rom. 3:10-11, 1 John 3:4). Because of our rule-breaking, we are condemned to face God's judgment and receive the just punishment for our sins (2 Cor. 5:10). However, Jesus came to earth and lived a faultless and righteous life, before being crucified on a Roman cross. On the cross, Jesus bore the punishment from God that should have been ours. He paid the penalty for our wrongdoings and wiped our legal debt clean so that, if we accept Jesus' sacrifice, we can be declared innocent and justified before the judgment seat of God (Rom. 3:25-26, 2 Cor. 5:21). Jesus received our condemnation so that we might receive His righteousness before God.

According to Georges, in shame-honour cultures, the gospel presentation that has most resonated with the culture is a little different. The most impactful gospel message in these contexts starts with human beings rebelling against God, who is our true and authoritative King and Father (Col. 1:21). In walking away from God, we have dishonoured His name and brought shame to our human race (Gen. 3:7, Luke 15:11-13). However, Jesus came from the place of highest honour to be born in the lowest squalor of a manger (Phil. 2:5-8). And He went on to live a humble life as a carpenter who associated with the most marginalised and rejected people in His society. Then Jesus died a criminal's death on the cross and in doing do, bore our shame and dishonour, as His executioners stripped, mocked, beat and hung him on a tree, and as His eternal Father turned His face away (Is. 53:3-4, Heb. 12:2). In bearing our shame on the cross, Jesus made the way by which we can be reconciled with our eternal Father, and so if we receive His Son, we can re-join God's royal family (Eph. 2:14-18, Luke 15:20-24).

Finally, Georges suggests that in fear-power cultures, the gospel message that has had the greatest influence begins with a world that is ruled by the Devil who has blinded sinners' eyes and imprisoned their hearts (Eph. 2:1-2, 2 Cor. 4:4). In response, Jesus, the omnipotent Son of God, came from heaven to earth to confront the power of Satan (1 John 3:8). In dying on the cross Jesus disarmed and defeated the spiritual powers of Satan, sin and death (Heb. 2:14-15). Three days later, Jesus rose victoriously from the grave, vindicating His authority as the rightful King of heaven and earth, and binding Satan for his inexorable destruction (Col. 2:15). Now, the risen Jesus offers us the chance to join Him and share in His victory, so that we can become conquering co-heirs with Christ (1 Cor. 15:57, Rom. 16:20).

Comments on *The 3D Gospel*

There are a few clarifying footnotes that are worth making following this brief summary of Georges' ideas in *The 3D Gospel*.

Firstly, as Georges himself acknowledges, this summation of world cultures is somewhat oversimplified. Clearly, there are more than three cultures in the world, and all world cultures will exhibit features of all three of Georges' cultural groups. Georges' book is more a simplified overview, rather than detailed analysis, of cultural anthropology.

Secondly, I do not think Georges is proposing that we ought to slice up the gospel and apportion different parts to different groups of people. We clearly should not just present people with the aspects of the gospel that we think they will want to hear. Rather, the Lausanne Covenant puts it well when it says: 'World evangelization requires the whole Church to take the *whole gospel* to the *whole world*'[2] (emphasis added). Christians clearly need to preach penal substitution in the East, and the victory of the cross in the West, and so on. To do otherwise would be to majorly shortchange listeners by presenting them with an incomplete gospel.

However, with these important caveats in place, Georges still makes an important and valuable point. Georges demonstrates that the gospel resonates with a culture when it speaks the language of the culture. The gospel captures the hearts and minds of listeners when it is presented in ways that are familiar to, and make sense in, the pre-existing cultural context of the listeners.

A Fourth Culture?

So where does that leave us, as those exploring how to speak for Jesus in our identity politics culture?

In some ways, identity politics culture exhibits features of all three cultural groups described by Georges. Many of the social justice campaigns are grounded in the principles of guilt and innocence, as activists fight for those who oppress and abuse others to be brought to justice under the law. But there are also the themes of shame and honour that run through many of the movements, such as the campaigns to replace the stigma and shame surrounding homosexuality with 'gay pride.' Furthermore, identity politics is influenced by the ideas of power and fear, such as the drive to empower minority identity groups to rise up and tear down the oppressive power structures in society.

In light of this, perhaps an argument can be made that in identity politics, we are seeing the emergence of a *fourth* culture. Perhaps we could call it an 'oppression-liberation' culture.

In this culture, societal wrongdoing is less framed in terms of rule-breaking, or family dishonour, or spiritual provocation, but rather in terms of complicity in oppression. Moreover, to gain status, reputation, public platform, and increasingly, job and social security, people must be seen to be joining the fight for the liberation of the oppressed. And in this oppression-liberation culture, those who fail to publicly join the fight for liberation are increasingly barred from accessing areas of public life.

The emergence of this fourth 'oppression-liberation' culture presents Christians with a unique opportunity. If Georges is right when he proposes that the gospel resonates with a culture when it speaks the language of the culture, then this is what Christians today should be trying to do. As we saw in Chapter 9, many of the principles of identity politics culture have deeply Christian roots. Modern discourse is permeated with words such as: freedom, liberation, justice, identity, diversity, equality, unity and peace. Therefore, perhaps we will see the gospel resonate with our culture when Christians begin to widely speak this sort of language. Identity politics brings a great opportunity for Christian evangelism, if we can develop a way of presenting the gospel that speaks the language of our culture.

So what would an 'oppression-liberation' gospel presentation actually look like? And how would it be different to the standard gospel presentations that we hear and use today? This brings us on to our second book that we are exploring in this chapter: *The Cross of Christ* by John Stott.

The Cross of Christ

We have met theologian John Stott a few times already in this book. Stott's probably most famous and celebrated book (of his many) is *The Cross of Christ*. In his endorsement, Vaughan Roberts says of *The Cross of Christ*: 'There is no more important theme than the cross of Christ, and there is no better book on the subject than John Stott's timeless classic.'[3] His authorship of *The Cross of Christ* is even mentioned on Stott's gravestone near his former writing retreat, The Hookses, in Wales.

In one of the central chapters of *The Cross of Christ*, Stott explores four key images that are used in the Bible to explain what Jesus' death on the cross accomplished. These are: justification, propitiation, reconciliation and redemption.[4] It is valuable to briefly unpack each of these images in turn.

1. Justification

As Stott explains, the image of justification brings us into the setting of the courtroom. We have all been found guilty of breaking God's laws and are therefore deserving of God's judicial punishment. However, on the cross, Jesus bore the penalty that should have been ours, so that through His death, we can be declared righteous, or 'justified,' before God the judge. As Paul writes in Romans 8:1-4:

> Therefore, there is now no condemnation for those who
> are in Christ Jesus, because through Christ Jesus the law
> of the Spirit who gives life has set you free from the law
> of sin and death… he condemned sin in the flesh, in
> order that the righteous requirement of the law might
> be fully met in us...

Jesus' death fulfilled the moral requirements of God's law that
we failed to meet, so that those who are in Christ will be legally
vindicated on the Day of Judgment.

2. Propitiation

Secondly, the image of propitiation brings us into the setting
of the temple. Our rebellion against God leads to us being the
subjects of God's holy and righteous wrath. God is angry at
our sin and rightly so. However, on the cross, Jesus stood in
our place and became the sacrifice which absorbed and averted
God's wrath against us. This is the image of the cross that the
Old Testament sacrifices of atonement (or 'propitiation') were
prophetically pointing towards. As Paul writes in Romans
3:25: 'God presented Christ as a sacrifice of atonement
[propitiation], through the shedding of his blood– to be received
by faith.' Therefore, the end result is that 'whoever believes in
the Son has eternal life, but whoever rejects the Son will not see
life, for God's wrath remains on them' (John 3:36).

3. Reconciliation

Thirdly the image of reconciliation brings us into the setting of the
home. In sinning against God, we have broken our relationship
with our good and faithful Heavenly Father, alienating ourselves
from Him. However, in dying on the cross, Jesus restored the
relationship and made the way by which we can return to God's
family. As Paul puts it in Romans 5:10: 'For if, while we were
God's enemies, we were reconciled to him through the death of
his Son, how much more, having been reconciled, shall we be

saved through his life!' One of the most powerful illustrations of the reconciliation accomplished at the cross was the curtain of the temple being torn in two as Jesus breathed His last breath on the cross (Matt. 27:50-51). The great dividing barrier between God's dwelling place in the temple and the people of the world outside was ripped apart so that now, through Jesus' death, all can come into the presence of God.

4. Redemption

Fourth and finally, Stott explores the image of redemption, bringing us into the setting of the marketplace. Through our rebellion against God, we have become enslaved and imprisoned by sin, and by ourselves we are unable to escape a life destined for the grave. However, in dying on the cross, Jesus bought us back at great cost to Himself, paying our ransom so that we might be set free to live for and with God. Stott points out that it was this redemptive image of the cross that was foreshadowed by the Old Testament redemption story of the Exodus, as God rescued His people from slavery and brought them through the wilderness into the Promised Land. As Peter writes in 1 Peter 1:18-19: 'For you know that it was not with perishable things such as silver or gold that you were redeemed from the empty way of life handed down to you from your ancestors, but with the precious blood of Christ, a lamb without blemish or defect.'

But this redemption is not just personal; it is also cosmic. Our personal redemption as Christians is part of the ultimate redemption story of the whole of creation. Creation is eagerly awaiting what Stott calls creation's 'day of redemption,' when it will be 'liberated from its bondage to decay and brought into the freedom and glory of the children of God' (Rom. 8:21).

Tell Me the Gospel

This is a very brief summary of just one key chapter of Stott's great work *The Cross of Christ* and there is obviously much more that can be said about the meaning and accomplishment of Jesus' death on the cross. But before we return to our central aim in this chapter, of developing a gospel presentation that speaks the language of our 'oppression-liberation' culture, it is helpful to first explore how each of these four images of the cross (justification, propitiation, reconciliation and redemption) are drawn upon by some of the currently most popular gospel tracts and evangelistic resources. Four popular resources that we are going to briefly look at are: *Two Ways To Live*, *Four Spiritual Laws*, the Alpha Course, and Christianity Explored.

Two Ways to Live

Two Ways to Live by Philip Jensen and Tony Payne is one of the most popular gospel tracts in the world, which summarises the gospel using six simple diagrams depicting: God's good creation, humans' rebellion against God, God's judgment on sin, Jesus' death on the cross, Jesus' resurrection, and the choice we have to accept or reject Jesus.

At the core of this gospel summary is the image of justification. *Two Ways to Live* explains the problem of sin in terms of our rejection of God's rule for our life, which lead us to a guilty standing before Him on the Day of Judgment. But, as the tract goes on: 'Jesus died as a substitute for rebels like us. He took upon himself the judgment and punishment that we deserved, by dying on the cross in our place. Death is the punishment for rebellion, and he died our death.'[5]

In *Two Ways to Live,* justification is the central image of the gospel presentation: Jesus died in our place and took the judgment and punishment we deserve.

Four Spiritual Laws

In his gospel tract *Have You Heard of the Four Spiritual Laws?* (often abbreviated to just 'Four Spiritual Laws') Bill Bright summarises the gospel in four 'spiritual laws':

1. God loves you and offers a wonderful plan for your life.
2. Man is sinful and separate from God. Therefore, he cannot know and experience God's love and plan for his life.
3. Jesus Christ is God's only provision for man's sin. Through Him you can know and experience God's love and plan for your life.
4. We must individually receive Jesus Christ as Savior and Lord; then we can know and experience God's love and plan for our lives.[6]

Have You Heard of the Four Spiritual Laws? focuses in part on the image of justification. Under Law 3, Bright explains that Jesus died on the cross 'in our place to pay the penalty for our sins.'[6]

But in addition, the tract also emphasises the image of reconciliation. Under Law 2, sin is explained as producing a great gulf between man and God. Bright then goes on to show that the death of Jesus is 'the only way to bridge this gulf.'[6] *Have You Heard of the Four Spiritual Laws?* introduces both the justification (Jesus paying the penalty for our wrongdoing) and reconciliation (Jesus rebuilding the broken relationship between us and God) of the cross.

Alpha

The image of reconciliation also features heavily in the 'Why Did Jesus Die?' talk in the Alpha Course. The Alpha Course is one of the most widely utilised evangelistic courses in the world, which started at Holy Trinity Brompton Church in London, and has since been translated into 112 different languages. In the Alpha film series, evangelist Nicky Gumbel explains the work of Jesus' death on the cross majoring on the image of reconciliation:

> Through the cross, partition between us and God has been removed. You can come home to God. St Paul puts it like this: God was in Christ reconciling the world to Himself... It's like the Prodigal Son – the story which

> Jesus told, of a son who'd gone away from home, who'd
> left his father, who'd wandered away- and then he comes
> back home.[7]

The video focusses on the reconciliation of the cross – how
Jesus' death made the way by which we can be brought back
to God and welcomed into His family, like the prodigal son in
Luke 15:11-32.

Christianity Explored

One of the most comprehensive evangelistic overviews of
the cross can be found in the popular Christianity Explored
course which began at All Souls Church Langham Place. In
Christianity Explored, (no doubt influenced by his mentor John
Stott) founder Rico Tice expounds the death of Jesus in Mark
15 under three headings that explore the images of propitiation,
justification and reconciliation in turn.

Firstly, under the heading 'God Was Angry,' Tice introduces
the image of propitiation. We are shown that because God is
good, He does not ignore sin, but instead gets righteously angry
at it (Rom. 2:5-6). Tice then goes on to explain that as Jesus
hung on the cross, darkness came over the whole of the land
(Mark 15:33), which 'tells us that God was acting in anger to
punish sin.'[8]

Secondly, under the title 'Jesus Was Abandoned,' Tice goes on
to describe the image of justification. Tice explains that as Jesus
cried out: 'My God, my God, why have you forsaken me?' (Mark
15:34), He 'was experiencing God's punishment… As Jesus died
on the cross, he willingly died for me, as my substitute, in my
place, taking the punishment I deserve.'[8]

Thirdly, under the title 'We Can Be Accepted,' Tice concludes
with the image of reconciliation as demonstrated by the curtain
in the temple being torn in two (Mark 15:38). Tice writes that
in tearing the temple curtain, 'God is saying that the way is now
open for us to enter his presence. The barriers are now down,

and there is nothing to prevent us from enjoying a relationship with him.'[8]

Under these three headings, Tice stacks up the three images of propitiation, justification and reconciliation, as we see Jesus bearing God's wrath in our place, taking the punishment for our sins, and tearing down the barrier between God and mankind.

The Missing Image

All the tracts and courses that we have briefly looked at above have been used by God to produce much gospel fruit around the world. Each gospel overview summarises the depths and breadths of the good news of Jesus in a way that is simple and accessible to seekers.

However, observant readers will have noticed that as we have surveyed some of the most popular evangelistic resources, there is one of Stott's images of the cross that has not yet made an appearance.[4] Justification is widely seen (at least in the global West) as the primary image of the cross and is at the heart of many evangelistic talks, tracts and courses. Reconciliation is also a commonly explored image in evangelistic contexts, including in the popular Alpha Course and Bill Bright's *Four Spiritual Laws*. Propitiation is classically seen as a less popular image amongst preachers and evangelists who can sometimes be apprehensive about preaching on God's wrath at sinful humanity. However, through resources such as Christianity Explored, which unashamedly explains God's wrath at sin that Jesus bore on the cross, many evangelical churches now regularly include the image of propitiation in their evangelism.

However, at least in my experience, the one image that is notably absent from many of our evangelistic talks, sermons and resources is that of *redemption*. It seems that the glorious truth – that through the death of Jesus we were bought at a great price out of slavery, oppression and imprisonment to sin, so that we may find true liberation in Christ – has become somewhat neglected in our evangelism.

This is pointedly ironic given that, as we have explored throughout Parts 1 and 3 of this book, the image of redemption is one of the core ideas at the heart of identity politics culture. In a culture that is longing for the oppressed and enslaved to gain freedom and liberation, the Church seems to be neglecting the precise gospel image that speaks directly into our cultural moment. Of course, I am not suggesting that we should preach less of justification, reconciliation or propitiation; these are all indispensable components of the gospel. But rather, we should simply not neglect the preaching of redemption, for this is the image that seems to most powerfully speak the language of our 'oppression-liberation' culture. Perhaps the rise of identity politics could become the catalyst that inspires Christians to preach *more of* the gospel.

Conclusion

The cultures of our world are numerous and varied, and the global Church is as diverse as the cultures it inhabits. As Jayson Georges argues in *The 3D Gospel*, the gospel has great power to resonate with a culture, particularly when it speaks the language of the culture. The gospel speaks impactfully of legal justification to guilt-innocence cultures, family reconciliation to shame-honour cultures, and cosmic victory to fear-power cultures.

In our modern culture of identity politics, we are perhaps seeing the emergence of a new type of culture: an 'oppression-liberation' culture. If this is true, then maybe we will see the gospel resonate with our identity politics culture when Christians start widely speaking the language of the culture.

As John Stott expounds in *The Cross of Christ*, the concept of 'liberation from oppression' has always been at the heart of the message of the cross. In dying on the cross Jesus gave us true and ultimate liberation. He broke the chains of sin and paid our ransom costs, so that we might be redeemed and experience the freedom that comes from living with and for our Creator. This is the image of the cross that seems to most powerfully speak the language of our identity politics culture. Yet ironically this is the image that seems most neglected in evangelistic talks and popular resources today. Perhaps unashamedly preaching the message of redemption may be one way that Christians can speak effectively for Jesus in a world of identity politics.

12. Living Redemptively

'…faith by itself, if it is not accompanied by action, is dead'
Apostle James, James 2:17

*'So what then is the mission of God's people? Surely it is to live as those
who have experienced [the] redeeming power of God.'*
Chris Wright, The Mission of God's People

In the opening chapter of his book *Integrity,* Jonathan Lamb
tells the true story of a man who was fired from his job at the
Coca-Cola bottling plant in California in 2003. He was not
fired because his work was sub-standard, nor because he was
persistently late for shifts, nor because he had a falling-out with
his boss. Rather, he was fired from his job at Coca-Cola because
he was caught, at work, drinking Pepsi! His physical actions did
not match the loyalty to Coca-Cola that he presumably declared
with his lips. Therefore, apparently, he had to go.

So far in this book, we have been exploring how Christians
can speak for Jesus in a world of identity politics. However, in
this final chapter, we are going to widen the lens and look briefly

at how we should *live* as Christians in the modern world. As the Bible says repeatedly, what we do with our hands and feet has the power to authenticate or nullify the message we preach with our mouths. James writes in James 2:14-17:

> What good is it, my brothers and sisters, if someone claims to have faith but has no deeds? Can such faith save them? Suppose a brother or a sister is without clothes and daily food. If one of you says to them, "Go in peace; keep warm and well fed," but does nothing about their physical needs, what good is it? In the same way, faith by itself, if it is not accompanied by action, is dead.

This is also a prominent theme in Jesus' Sermon on the Mount. In Matthew 7:21-23, Jesus gives this unsettling warning:

> Not everyone who says to me, "Lord, Lord," will enter the kingdom of heaven, but only the one who does the will of my Father who is in heaven. Many will say to me on that day, "Lord, Lord, did we not prophesy in your name and in your name drive out demons and in your name perform many miracles?" Then I will tell them plainly, "I never knew you. Away from me, you evildoers!"

Jesus says that authentic, saving faith in Him is demonstrated not by prophesying, casting out evil, or even calling Jesus 'Lord.' Rather, true faith manifests in *doing* the will of the Father.

Clearly, the topic of Christian living in the modern world is an enormous one on which hundreds of books have been written. In this chapter, our aim is to pull out just one thread as we begin to answer the question: how should we *live* for Jesus in a world of identity politics?

Living Redemptively

As we saw in the last chapter, Christians are called to preach a redemptive gospel. We have been bought out of slavery to sin, through the ransom payment of the blood of Jesus, so that we may experience true liberation as those following the way of our Creator. As we suggested in the last chapter, this is a message that resonates with our identity politics culture. However, redemption is not something we should merely preach; it is also something we should live out. As Christians, we are called to live redemptively.

One theologian who explains this well is Chris Wright. In his book *The Mission of God's People*, Wright lays out twelve facets of Christian mission which range from creation care, to being a blessing to the nations, to proclaiming the gospel, to praising God. All of this is in answer to Wright's opening question behind Christian mission: 'Who are we and what are we here for?'[1]

In one chapter, Wright unpacks how Christians are 'people who are redeemed for redemptive living.'[1] He begins the chapter by exploring the Bible's overarching redemption story, beginning with the Exodus as we see God's people being rescued out of slavery in Egypt by the blood of the Passover Lamb. He then goes on to show how the Exodus was a miniature foreshowing of the ultimate redemption story that was fulfilled in Jesus' death on the cross – what Wright calls: 'the grand exodus par excellence.'[1]

What then is the Christian's mission, as one who is redeemed by Christ out of slavery to sin and death? Wright answers: 'Surely it is to live as those who have experienced that redeeming power of God already, and whose lives – individual and corporate – are signposts to the ultimate liberation of all creation and humanity from every form of oppression and slavery.'[1]

God's people are called to live out their redemption, by living redemptively to others.

Wright goes on to give four ways that the people of God are commanded in Scripture to live out their redemption: slave release, generosity, Jubilee and debt forgiveness. It is valuable to briefly look at each of these in turn.

1. Slave Release

In Exodus 21, immediately after the Ten Commandments, God gives the Israelites the framework by which Hebrew slaves were to be liberated. Exodus 21:1-3 reads: 'If you buy a Hebrew servant [or 'slave' in ESV], he is to serve you for six years. But in the seventh year, he shall go free, without paying anything. If he comes alone, he is to go free alone; but if he has a wife when he comes, she is to go with him.'

The Israelites were commanded to live out their redemption from slavery in Egypt by redeeming and freeing their Hebrew slaves upon their seventh year of service. As Wright points out:

> it is not surprising to find that the first laws given to Israel – a bunch of escaped slaves – immediately after the Ten Commandments, have to do with the way they were to treat those who, in their own society, would find themselves in some form of bonded labour.[1]

Although this is not the place for a thorough examination of the topic of slavery in the Bible, there are nonetheless a few brief clarifying points worth mentioning here.

Firstly, as theologian Gordon Wenham explains in his commentary on Leviticus, the system of slavery existed in Israelite society as a last resort for those who found themselves in debt that they could not pay.[2] Wenham draws parallels between this and the modern prison system.[2] (Prisons themselves would have been clearly impossible in a community of tent-dwellers.) This was very different to the slavery experienced by the Israelites in Egypt or perpetrated during the Trans-Atlantic Slave Trade. Kidnapping people to sell them into forced labour is explicitly prohibited in Scripture (Ex. 21:16, 1 Tim. 1:10) and clear laws were set in place to protect slaves from abuse (Ex. 21:20, Eph. 6:9).

Secondly, it is germane to acknowledge that there were different laws for slaves from other nations (Lev. 25:44-46), although the blanket safeguards against mistreatment still applied (Ex. 21:16, 20). Wenham suggests that the specific commands around Hebrew slave release were given to the Israelites to demonstrate and remind them of their identity as the redeemed people of God[2], and therefore their motivation to live redemptively.

Thirdly, although Scripture does not call for the immediate end of the system of slavery, it does lay down the foundational principles of equality, dignity and redemption that set the trajectory towards abolitionism. Once the New Testament declared: 'There is neither Jew nor Gentile, neither slave nor free... for you are all one in Christ Jesus' (Gal. 3:28), the framework was in place for William Wilberforce and the Clapham Sect to lead the abolitionist movement in the UK, not in spite of their Christian faith, but because of it.

2. Generosity

Secondly, the Israelites were to live redemptively by showing generosity to the poor and oppressed. We read in Deuteronomy 15:13-15:

> And when you release them [slaves], do not send them away empty-handed. Supply them liberally from your flock, your threshing floor and your winepress. Give to them as the LORD your God has blessed you. Remember that you were slaves in Egypt and the LORD your God redeemed you. That is why I give you this command today.

The Israelites were not just commanded to release slaves, but also to bless them through the generous giving of resources and gifts. Note that there is no upper limit for this generosity in these verses, other than to bless 'liberally.'

This command is framed as a natural consequence of the lavish blessings God poured out on the Israelites. Generosity is not meant to be motivated by reluctant obligation, but rather by an overflowing of gratitude to God. God's people are to mirror the generosity of God through generosity to others – particularly those in greatest financial need.

We see a New Testament example of this in Acts 2, when we read that in the Early Church: 'All the believers were together and had everything in common. They sold property and possessions to give to anyone who had need' (Acts 2:44-45). These first century Christians were not just generous with their spare change; they sold their personal properties and possessions in order to comprehensively provide for the needs of others.

3. Jubilee

The third way that the Israelites were to live out their redemption, that Wright gives, is found in the Year of Jubilee. In Leviticus 25, God commands the Israelites:

> Consecrate the fiftieth year and proclaim liberty throughout the land to all its inhabitants. It shall be a jubilee for you; each of you is to return to your family property and to your own clan...
>
> ...If one of your fellow Israelites becomes poor and sells some of their property, their nearest relative is to come and redeem what they have sold... But if they do not acquire the means to repay, what was sold will remain in the possession of the buyer until the Year of Jubilee. It will be returned in the Jubilee, and they can then go back to their property. (Lev 25:10, 25-28)

Every forty-nine years, any land and property that was bought or sold in Israel was to revert back to its original owner. Traded land and property were essentially rented for a maximum of forty-nine years through one-off advance payments.[2] As Wright explains, the Jubilee Year was designed to prevent poor people descending down a 'spiral of debt, poverty and dispossession'[1] whilst the rich became richer. Regular financial redemption of the poor was fundamental to the structure of Israelite society, for every forty-nine years, everyone's financial slate was wiped clean.

4. Forgiveness

Wright's fourth and final way God's people should live out their redemption is by forgiving debtors.

In Matthew 18, Peter asks Jesus: 'Lord, how many times shall I forgive my brother or sister who sins against me?' (Matt. 18:21). Jesus responds by telling the story of a servant who owes his master a large amount of money he cannot pay back. His master takes pity on him and forgives his debt. But then, the servant goes and finds another servant who owes him a smaller amount, and when he cannot pay, he has this second servant thrown in prison (Matt. 18:23-35).

Jesus' parable is a striking illustration of the absurdity of someone being forgiven much but yet not being willing to show forgiveness to others. This parable may have a literal application for Christians who are owed money by people who will never realistically be able to pay it back. However, the clear broader application is that Christians ought to forgive those who sin against us, for we have had our sins forgiven at the cross. As C. S. Lewis pithily remarks in *The Weight of Glory*: 'To be a Christian means to forgive the inexcusable because God has forgiven the inexcusable in you.'[4]

Into the Present

As Wright shows in *The Mission of God's People,* throughout the Bible, God's people are called to redemptive living. Those redeemed by the grace of God are then called to liberate those who have been enslaved, provide generously for those who have fallen on hard times, fight for justice for the oppressed, and redeem those who have found themselves in poverty, debt or deprivation.

So what does living redemptively look like today? How can Christians, particularly in the UK, not just preach a redemptive gospel, but live it out as well?

Of course, modern UK society is a very different context to the Israelites entering the Promised Land or the early Christians living under the Roman Empire. As we saw in Chapter 2, slavery was outlawed in the UK in 1833. Furthermore, in the UK, we have a publicly funded National Health Service that provides healthcare to everyone, free at the point of need, and irrespective of the patient's social or financial background. And we have a welfare state that apportions money from general taxation to provide financial protection and assistance for the poor, unemployed and vulnerable.

One of the potential consequences of living in a country that has a well-resourced and wide-reaching healthcare system and welfare state is that providing for the poor and vulnerable becomes a secondary priority for the Church and individual Christians. This practical redemption can end up being seen as 'contracted out' to the State, leaving the Church to just concentrate on evangelism and discipling Christians. Ironically, I suspect this is a particular risk in well-resourced, middle-class churches.

It is worth pointing out here that the modern healthcare and welfare systems have Christian historic foundations. Christians were instrumental in the invention of the hospital system, as John Wyatt explains:

> As Christianity spread through Graeco-Roman society… a central peculiarity of these Christians was that they cared for the "riff-raff"… It is not surprising that the early Christians built hospitals, including distinctly dangerous places, such as specialist hospitals for plague victims and leprosy sufferers. Even the word "hospital" has Christian roots. It comes from the Latin "hospes," meaning "guest." A hospital is a place where we practise

hospitality, neighbour-love to strangers, a bizarre concept
first introduced by one Jesus of Nazareth.[5]

One of the founding pioneers of the modern welfare state
was Archbishop of Canterbury William Temple. In his Henry
Scott Holland lectures in 1928, Temple introduced the concept
of the 'welfare state.' Then in his 1942 book *Christianity and
Social Order*, Temple laid out his framework for the welfare state
which, rooted in Christian theology, proposed a range of ideas
including: a national basic level of income, universal access to
education for children, two days protected leisure time in the
working week, and guaranteed freedom of speech, assembly and
association[6]. Temple's writing and ideas greatly influenced both
the religious and political worlds of his day and beyond. In the
preface of the 1976 edition of *Christianity and Social Order*, former
UK Prime Minister Edward Heath writes: 'Temple's impact on
my generation was immense… His personal influence was not
limited to those of his own way of thinking. It extended to those
who held no religious belief and to those whose political views
did not march with his own.'[6]

The modern health and welfare systems, that are now integral
building blocks of UK society, have deeply Christian roots.
Because of these, many of the social, financial and health needs
of the poor and vulnerable are met, at least to some degree, by
the State. However, this should not lead to complacency amongst
Christians. Rather it ought to make Christians more intentionally
vigilant of the needs of the poor, oppressed and vulnerable in
our society – and there are many.

Opportunities for the Church

So how can the Church live out a redemptive gospel in a wealthy
modern society like the UK?

Despite the existence and successes of the NHS and welfare
state, it does not require much research to begin to identify a
huge number of unmet social, financial and physical needs in

UK society, and therefore a whole range of opportunities for redemptive living. Here are a few statistics that demonstrate this:

- The Office of National Statistics in 2014 estimated there were between 10,000 and 13,000 potential victims of modern slavery living in the UK, including victims of labour exploitation, sexual exploitation and those trafficked for organ harvesting.[7]
- According to the government's report, the estimated number of rough sleepers in the UK on a single night in Autumn 2020 was 2,688, of which nearly half were in London and the South East of the England.[8]
- The Institute for Fiscal Studies reported that in 2019-2020, relative child poverty in the UK reached 31 per cent, which was a 4 per cent increase since 2011-2012.[9]
- In December 2020, the international children's charity Unicef announced that, for the first time in its over seventy-year history, it was going to fund schemes in the UK, to provide food for children at risk of hunger during the Autumn and Winter periods.[10]
- According to The Department of Education's report, on 30th June 2021, there were 2,040 children in the UK awaiting adoption. Over half of these children had been waiting over eighteen months.[11]

The COVID-19 pandemic exacerbated many of the existing poverties and inequalities in UK society. Those who were already socially, financially and physically vulnerable prior to the pandemic were often amongst the worst affected by the physical consequences of COVID-19,[12] and the social and economic impacts of the lockdowns and government restrictions.[13] COVID-19 also highlighted the importance of ordinary citizens looking out for the needs of others in their community. During the heights of the COVID waves, it often fell to communities, charities and the kindness of individuals to do things such as: shopping for the self-isolating, reaching out to the lonely and bereaved, financially supporting those who had been made redundant, or raising the morale of the healthcare workers battling the virus on the frontline.

All this goes to show that even in a wealthy country that has well-developed and well-funded health and welfare systems, there is still a great need for the Church to act redemptively. As those redeemed by God from slavery to sin and death and brought into the riches of the Kingdom of God, the Church should likewise work to redeem those around us. The Church should be the first to offer love, care, help and support to the poor and vulnerable – be they the homeless, the trafficked, the unemployed, the hungry or the lonely.

Furthermore, in the gospels we see that Jesus was particularly concerned with the needs of vulnerable children. We read in Matthew 19:13-14:

'Then people brought little children to Jesus for him to place his hands on them and pray for them. But the disciples rebuked them. Jesus said, "Let the little children come to me, and do not hinder them, for the kingdom of heaven belongs to such as these."'

Therefore, it ought to be a priority for the Church to care for children like Jesus did. Churches should be working to ensure that the children in their communities do not go hungry, and the thousands of children awaiting adoption and fostering find safe and loving homes.

Whatever our local church context, there will inevitably be a range of opportunities for the Church to act redemptively in response to the needs of its community. But we will only be able to do this if we are willingly to listen carefully to the struggles and needs of those around us. Here is how pastor Tim Keller describes how his New York church approached the needs of his community:

> When Redeemer Church purchased property in a neighborhood in Manhattan, we visited both with

the neighborhood's city councilwoman and the local community board. Our questions were: What are the needs here that you and the community feel are both chronic and acute? What could we do that would make this neighborhood a better place to live in?... Everyone we have approached has been surprised that a church would even ask. Ordinarily, churches and other religious institutions assume they know best what the community needs.[14]

I do also believe that there is a place for Christian activism and political lobbying. As has hopefully become apparent throughout this book, there are certain aspects of identity politics culture that run contrary to biblical teaching. However, this should not stop us from campaigning for equality and justice. Furthermore, we should use the still relatively powerful voice of the Church in the UK to advocate for the vulnerable and sinned-against, including victims of prejudice and discrimination.

The Church is called to be a redemptive institution in its actions as well as its words. And in the UK, the redemptive needs are great.

Opportunities for Christians

But redemptive living is not just a corporate calling for the Church at large. We, individual Christians, are also each called to live redemptively in the contexts and circumstances God places us in every day. Whatever stage of life we are at, and whatever circles we move in, there will inevitably be opportunities to live redemptively towards those around us. Here are three brief examples.

Firstly, all of us will, at some point, rub shoulders with people who have been victims of injustice through no fault of their own. Therefore, we will all have opportunity to be what author Mark Greene calls 'a mouthpiece for truth and justice.'[15] These are not always the major injustices that make the news or go viral on Twitter. But, as Greene writes in his book *Fruitfulness on the Frontline*:

> Speaking up for truth and justice isn't just about such big challenges. What do we do when there's a succulent morsel of gossip whisking its titillating way round our sports club, or when someone in the family is being blamed for something they didn't do and they don't know how to stick up for themselves?... Or what do we do when the wrong person is taking the blame at work, or when the wrong person is getting the credit?[15]

When those around us are wronged or blamed unjustly, because of malice, ignorance or even accident, therein lies the opportunity to act redemptively by being a mouthpiece for justice.

Secondly and more broadly, most of us will interact frequently with others who are junior to us in our workplace, or less respected than us in our social context, or less popular than us in our classroom, or less successful than us in our field, or less powerful than us in our society. Therefore all of us will have opportunities to show practical, redemptive love by respecting, upholding and valuing those less privileged than ourselves. Being redeemed by Jesus should have a tangible impact on the way a senior colleague treats their junior, or an employer treats their employee, or a straight-A student treats their struggling classmate, or a pastor treats their poorest parishioner.

Thirdly, Christians ought to be redemptive with our finances. As Chris Wright points out, the lavish generosity of God should lead Christians to be generous to others, particularly those less well-off than ourselves.[1] When we hear that someone in our church has fallen on financially hard times, how quickly do we open our wallet or load up our banking app? How many charities, ministries and organisations who care for the poor and vulnerable do we support enthusiastically with our lips, but not with our cash? And most brutally simply of all, how much of our money do we spend on ourselves, compared with on other people?

These are just three of numerous possible ways ordinary Christians can live redemptively in our day-to-day lives. To be clear, we should not embark on this redemptively living out of compulsion or guilt. Rather it should come as a natural overflowing of the undeserved and generous redemption we have received from God.

Opportunities for the Gospel

We have so far seen in this chapter that there are many opportunities for the Church at large, and individual Christians in their own contexts, to live out their redemption by living redemptively towards others. But it is apt to end this chapter where it began, by looking at how our actions impact the way our gospel message is received.

Throughout church history, the redemptive actions of the Church have gone hand-in-hand with its preaching of the gospel. For example, it was the combination of words and actions that led to the explosive growth of the Church in the first and second centuries. The second-century author Tertullian observed that the early Church made itself distinctive to the pagan culture around it through its radical care and compassion for the poor and vulnerable. Tertullian writes:

> For they [the church's funds] are not taken thence and spent on feasts, and drinking-bouts, and eating-houses, but to support and bury poor people, to supply the wants of boys and girls destitute of means and parents, and of old persons confined now to the house; such, too, as have suffered shipwreck; and if there happen to be any in the mines, or banished to the islands, or shut up in the prisons, for nothing but their fidelity to the cause of God's Church, they become the nurslings of their confession.[16]

As Professor of Social Sciences Rodney Stark points out in his book *The Rise of Christianity*, this care and compassion for the poor, oppressed and suffering drew people to the early Church-especially during times of pandemic.[17] This became one of the key contributing factors to the rise of Christianity in the Ancient Graeco-Roman world.[17] Christians should live redemptively not only as a natural outworking of our personal redemption story, nor simply because Jesus commanded and exemplified it – although these would be good enough reasons in themselves. Christians also should live redemptively because it authenticates the redemptive gospel we preach. Redemptive living should not be seen as a secondary priority to evangelism – it should be seen as an intrinsic part of it.

Conclusion

This book has been all about how Christians can speak for Jesus in a world of identity politics. But in this final chapter, we have explored one way in which our redemptive gospel should manifest in the way we live. Throughout Scripture, God's people are taught that in light of their redemption from slavery in Egypt, and ultimately from slavery to sin and death, they should respond by living redemptively towards others. Christians are called to liberate those who have been enslaved, provide generously for those who have fallen on hard times, fight for justice for the oppressed, and redeem those who have found themselves in poverty, debt or deprivation.

In modern UK society, we should rejoice and praise God for all the good that is done by the health service and welfare state, which themselves have deeply Christian roots. However, there are still great redemptive needs in our society and therefore many opportunities for the Church at large and Christians individually to live redemptively. Furthermore, living redemptively authenticates the gospel message of redemption that we should be preaching. Our culture not only needs to hear of the redemptive gospel, but to see it too.

Conclusion

'His kingdom will not be destroyed, his dominion will never end.'
King Darius, Daniel 6:26

Nearly seventy years on from when Billy Graham touched down in the UK for his first Haringey Crusade, the UK is a very different place. Identity politics has begun to affect and shape nearly every area of modern life, from birth certificates and nursery education, through to school dances and university lectures, to football matches and cricket rules, to medical journals and maternity care, to church policies and evangelistic events.

The identity politics revolution is driven by a powerful grand narrative: that of the oppressed groups, waking up to their oppression, and then rising up to fight against their societal oppressors. However, in this grand cultural story, Christians have found themselves on the wrong side of history. In the eyes of our culture, Christians are often seen as the oppressors: the homophobic, transphobic, sexist, racist, anti-liberal, anti-progressive bigots who need to be overthrown.

Unsurprisingly many Christians have not taken kindly to being labelled as the oppressors in this grand cultural narrative.

Some Christians have responded by mirroring the rhetoric and campaigns of the social justice movements, whilst others have set out to debate the issues and publicly argue the case for Christianity. However, in a society of increasing political hostility and 'cancel culture,' mirroring and arguing are often proving ineffectual at best and destructive at worst. This has led to many Christians retreating from the hostility and simply ignoring the revolution outside our doors. Except it is not outside our doors. For better or worse, identity politics is now shaping the lives of Christians, the policies of our churches and the ways people respond to our evangelism. We cannot keep on ignoring the revolution happening around us.

Perhaps we need to re-think the way we engage our culture with the gospel. Perhaps it is time for a new type of apologetics.

In a society in which charismatic preachers and astute apologists are increasingly cancelled by the culture, one thing we can do is tell stories. After all, you cannot argue against a story. In this book, we have put forward the case that Christians should respond to the narratives of identity politics by telling a more powerful counter-narrative: a better story. This may not be as difficult as it first appears, given that many of the ideas and principles that drive the identity politics movements have deeply biblical historic foundations, such as: freedom, liberation, justice, identity, diversity, equality, unity and peace. If Christians in the pulpit, on the University campuses, and in ordinary day-to-day life, can grasp this 'oppression-liberation' cultural language, and show that the gospel provides the true and ultimate better story, perhaps we will then see the gospel resonate with our modern culture. Perhaps this is how we should speak for Jesus in a world of identity politics.

His Kingdom Will Not Be Destroyed

As we draw this book to a close, I would like to end with some final thoughts from a famous passage in the Old Testament.

The book of Daniel tells the story of how the prophet Daniel and his friends were carried off into exile in Babylon whilst the Babylonian army razed Jerusalem to the ground. Daniel settles in Babylon and makes his way up the career ladder of the Babylonian civil service. Then in Daniel 5, the Babylonian Empire is conquered and taken over by the Empire of the Medes and the Persians, led by Darius the Mede.

We then come to Daniel 6, and we meet Daniel as a senior and trusted administer under King Darius. However, probably motivated by a mixture of jealousy and racism, Daniel's colleagues seek to depose him from his position. However, unable to find any evidence of corruption or negligence that they could use against him, Daniel's colleagues resort to targeting his faith in God. They successfully persuade King Darius to issue a royal decree that 'anyone who prays to any god or human being during the next thirty days, except to you, Your Majesty, shall be thrown into the lions' den' (Dan. 6:7).

Nevertheless, Daniel continues his routine of praying to God three times a day at his window facing the remains of Jerusalem. Daniel is soon arrested for disobeying the king's decree and, despite protestations from the king, is thrown into the lions' den. It is at this point that we pick up the story in Daniel 6:19-26:

> At the first light of dawn, the king got up and hurried to the lions' den. When he came near the den, he called to Daniel in an anguished voice, "Daniel, servant of the living God, has your God, whom you serve continually, been able to rescue you from the lions?"

> Daniel answered, "May the king live forever! My God sent his angel, and he shut the mouths of the lions. They have not hurt me, because I was found innocent in his sight. Nor have I ever done any wrong before you, Your Majesty."

The king was overjoyed and gave orders to lift Daniel out of the den...

...Then King Darius wrote to all the nations and peoples of every language in all the earth:

May you prosper greatly! I issue a decree that in every part of my kingdom people must fear and reverence the God of Daniel.

"For he is the living God
  and he endures forever;
his kingdom will not be destroyed,
  his dominion will never end."

As our journey through the culture of identity politics comes in to land, there are three brief points from this story in Daniel 6 that are valuable to end on.

1. God's Kingdom Will Be Opposed

Daniel 6 mirrors a similar story in Daniel 3, when Daniel's Jewish friends are thrown into a fiery furnace for refusing to worship an image that Babylonian King Nebuchadnezzar had set up. And of course, these are two of countless examples from Scripture and church history of God's people facing the most severe of persecution because of their faith. Throughout history, persecution has been the normal experience of the followers of God. As Paul says in 2 Timothy 3:12-13: 'In fact, everyone who wants to live a godly life in Christ Jesus will be persecuted, while evildoers and impostors will go from bad to worse, deceiving and being deceived.' Peter goes even further and commands the Christians scattered by persecution across Asia Minor: 'do not be surprised at the fiery ordeal that has come on you to test you, as though something strange were happening to you' (1 Pet. 4:12).

Opposition and persecution are not reserved for the professional missionaries and evangelists, or those who enjoy stoking Twitter storms. Persecution, in some form, is the expected experience for all those who want to live for Jesus. In fact, being cancelled on Twitter, being de-platformed in universities, or even losing a job for being Christian is still relatively minor persecution in comparison to the threats to life and liberty that Daniel, Paul, Peter and many of our Christian forerunners have faced down the centuries. That is not to say that we should not be winsome, strategic, wise and careful in our evangelism. But we should also not be surprised when we meet opposition.

2. God Will Be With His People

So firstly, God's Kingdom will be opposed. But secondly, God will always be with His people. As Daniel announces from within the lions' den: 'God sent his angel, and he shut the mouths of the lions' (Dan. 6:22). Daniel survived the jaws of the lions because God was with him in the den.

Today, Christians worship that same God. We do not follow a distant God who just agrees to beam us up to heaven when we die. Christians follow a God who promises to be with us in the trials and troubles of this life. But even more astonishingly, He is a God who came from heaven to earth to be born into the mess and turbulence of human culture. Then, when He ascended to heaven, Jesus promised the Holy Spirit who comes to dwell in all those who put their faith in Jesus. God, by His Spirit, is always with His children.

Living as a Christian in a culture that increasingly sees Christianity as oppressive and bigoted can feel lonely and isolated. It is in these sorts of times that Christians need to remind ourselves and each other of the eternal presence of God. God is with us when we are cancelled, marginalised or persecuted for our faith. This should be a source of great peace and confidence for Christians. As the quote that is often attributed to abolitionist Frederick Douglass says: 'One and God make a majority.'

3. God's Gospel Will Prevail

As the story of Daniel and the lions' den shows, God's Kingdom will be opposed, and God will be with His people. Third and finally, God's Kingdom will be victorious and His gospel will prevail. Following Daniel's miraculous emergence from the lions' den, Darius, the pagan king, then proclaims the remarkable declaration that the God of Israel 'is the living God and he endures forever; his kingdom will not be destroyed, his dominion will never end' (Dan. 6:26). Kings will come and go, and cultures will rise and fall, but God's Kingdom will ultimately prevail and His dominion will last forever.

In the New Testament, Jesus makes a similar declaration when he says to Peter that even 'the gates of Hades will not overcome' the building of His Church (Matt. 16:18). When the Church appears bruised, marginalised or even fading into cultural irrelevance, Jesus' promise is that the Kingdom of God will keep growing and the gospel will keep going. The growth of God's Kingdom is not dependent on the skill of our apologetics, or the articulateness of our talks, or the bravery with which we face down persecution, although these are all good things. It is only in the power of God that souls are saved and the gospel spreads.

So as we set out to engage our modern culture with the gospel, we should first begin on our knees – in prayer to the living God who 'is able to do immeasurably more than all we ask or imagine, according to his power that is at work within us' (Eph. 3:20), and who commands us to pray 'let your kingdom come' (Matt. 6:10).

God's Kingdom will prevail, and it is this assurance that makes it worth speaking for Jesus in a world of identity politics.

Appendix: A Word on Youth Ministry

I felt it worthwhile to give a few extra comments specifically to readers involved in ministry to children and young people. I am not just referring here to youth ministers and volunteer church youth leaders. I would include those with the high calling of raising children in the faith within the home. And perhaps most strategically of all, I would also include Christians involved in teaching and caring for children and young people in the secular education and care sectors.

Throughout this book, I have tried to impress the urgency with which Christians need to think about, engage with, and respond to the identity politics revolution. I would suggest that this urgency is most acutely seen within ministry to young people.

Young people are the most likely to be influenced and shaped by campaigns and ideologies propagated on social media. They are the group most immediately impacted by education policy changes, including in the areas of sex, relationships and gender. And they are going through highly formative years in which their surrounding cultures and social circumstances can set the trajectory for the rest of their lives. The most impressionable people in our society are the ones most saturated in identity politics culture.

Furthermore, for teenagers and those younger than them, the era in which Christianity and Christian values were seen as mainstream, or even generally acceptable in UK society, is effectively ancient history. Our postmodern, post-Christian culture is the only culture they have known.

And yet, at least from my anecdotal experience, the one place where young people are usually not receiving teaching about identity politics is in church. Young people are being immersed in identity politics culture by their schoolmates, teachers, social media, films, television, celebrities and role models. But where is the Christian voice? Where are those questioning the narratives of our modern culture and telling young people the better gospel story?

How this can be done will differ between contexts.

Church pastors and youth workers should not hide from issues such as sexuality, gender and race, but teach on them directly. The very legitimate desires to be careful, wise and loving, particularly with young people, should not result in church leaders simply ignoring some of the biggest issues facing those under their spiritual care.

In the secular classroom context, there is an even greater delicacy with which Christian teachers need to approach these issues. It would often be inappropriate for teachers to simply teach Christian values from the front of a lesson. However, teachers can cultivate discussions that encourage young people to think critically about the cultural narratives that they are consuming. For example, they can pose discussion questions such as: 'What would a truly tolerant society look like?' or 'What does it really mean to be free?'

I hope the contents of this book are helpful for those thinking about how to engage with young people on these issues. Ministries to children and young people are high and important callings, particularly in today's culture. As Proverbs 22:6 reminds us: 'Start children off on the way they should go, and even when they are old they will not turn from it.'

Glossary

Affirmative Action – *see Position Discrimination*

Cancel Culture – the term used to describe the culture in which views that are deemed to be offensive or 'politically incorrect' are ostracised or silenced.

Conversion Therapy (also 'Reparative Therapy') – the controversial practice of using physical, psychological and/or spiritual interventions with the aim of changing a person's sexual orientation or gender identity.

Critical Theory – the political philosophy which originated in the Frankfurt School, that frames society as ultimately a power struggle between oppressor and oppressed groups and aims to reveal and deconstruct the institutionalised power structures that propagate oppression.

Culture Wars – the term used to describe the verbal, and sometimes physical, hostility that arises when the ideologies of different identity groups clash.

De-Transitioner – someone who has transitioned from one gender to another, but then concludes that the decision was wrong for them, and so has begun to transition back.

Equity – the equal distribution of markers of success or achievement across different demographic groups.

Expressive Individualism – the idea that meaning to life can be found through the external expression of internal emotions, desires and convictions.

Gender Dysphoria – distress or discomfort associated with someone's gender identity being different to their biological sex.

Gender Fluid – someone whose gender identity is not fixed, but changes over time or from day to day.

Gender Identity – the gender that someone self-identifies as.

Gender Non-Binary – someone who does not self-identify as male or female.

Gender Non-Conforming – someone who does not conform to societal binary gender norms.

Gesture Politics – the pejorative term used to refer to activism that simply deploys symbolic gestures rather than political action.

Heteronormativity – the view that heterosexuality is the normative framework for all romantic and sexual relationships.

Identity Politics – the phenomenon by which people have begun to move away from the traditional political divisions of 'left versus right wing,' or 'conservative vs liberal,' and have begun instead to coalesce around identity groups, such as race, sexuality, gender and age.

Intersectionality – the view in which individuals who fall into more than one minority category experience a unique type of oppression and have an especially important voice.

Intersex – the term used to describe the various conditions where a person's anatomy is not easily classified as biologically male or female.

Jim Crow Laws – the laws that were instituted in former Confederate states following the end of the American Civil War, which segregated black and white citizens in public institutions.

Male Privilege – the term used to describe the system of advantages men appear to receive merely by virtue of being male.

Mansplaining – the term used to describe a man patronisingly or condescendingly explaining something to a woman.

Patriarchy – the term used to describe the societal or institutional structures that are viewed as empowering and elevating men whilst oppressing and disadvantaging women.

Political Correctness – the term used to describe language and expressed viewpoints that are intended to be inoffensive, particularly to minority groups.

Populism – the political approach that aims to galvanise ordinary, working-class citizens who feel that their identities are being disregarded by the ruling establishment classes.

Positive Discrimination (also 'Affirmative Action,' US) – the system of ensuring demographic representation in an institution through quotas or requirements that systematically advantage minority groups.

Puberty Blockers – medications that are used to delay the development of puberty, with the intention of allowing young people more time to explore their gender identity.

Social Justice Movements – the organised actions and activism of groups campaigning against societal and institutional injustices, particularly injustices against oppressed minority groups.

Social Justice Warriors – the name sometimes given to activists who are involved in the campaigns of the social justice movements.

Suffrage – the legal right to vote in political elections.

TERF (Trans-Exclusionary Radical Feminist) – the pejorative name given to feminists who fail to include trans rights in their campaigns or advocacy.

Trans – abbreviation of 'Transgender.'

Transgender – the term used for someone whose gender identity is different to their biological sex.

Transgender Female – someone who is biologically male but self-identifies as female.

Transgender Male – someone who is biologically female but self-identifies as male.

Toxic Masculinity – the term used to describe stereotypically masculine traits that propagate a patriarchal culture, such as bullying, aggression and misogyny.

White Privilege – the term used to refer to the system of advantages and benefits that white people appear to receive simply by virtue of them being white.

Woke – the term originally used in Black American folk music to describe the need for minorities to be vigilant to the systems and people that oppress them.

References

Introduction

1. Peck, A. Billy Graham: His Impact on Britain. *Premier Christianity* (2001).
2. Stott, J. *The Contemporary Christian: An Urgent Plea for Double Listening.* (Inter-Varsity Press, 1992).

Chapter 1: Feminism

1. Stott, J. *The Contemporary Christian: An Urgent Plea for Double Listening.* (Inter-Varsity Press, 1992).
2. Richardson, M. Miss Richardson's Statement. *The Times* (1914).
3. Beauvoir, S. de. *The Second Sex.* (Vintage Classics, 1949).
4. Greer, G. *The Female Eunuch.* (Harper Perennial, 1970).
5. Firestone, S. *The Dialectic of Sex.* (Farrar Straus & Giroux, 1970).
6. ONS. Gender pay gap in the UK: 2021 (2021).
7. GEO. Gender Equality Monitor: Tracking progress on gender equality. *Gov. Equal. Off.* (2019).
8. Bates, L. How to convince sceptics of the value of feminism. *The Economist* (2018).

9. SlutWalk London. Slutwalk London 2012 (invitation webpage) (2012).

10. Valenti, J. SlutWalks and the future of feminism. *Washington Post* (2011).

11. Kantor, J. & Twohey, M. Harvey Weinstein Paid Off Sexual Harassment Accusers for Decades. *New York Times* (2017).

12. Carlsen, A. *et al.* #MeToo Brought Down 201 Powerful Men. Nearly Half of Their Replacements Are Women. *New York Times* (2018).

13. Lord's. MCC to use the Term 'Batters' Throughout the Laws of Cricket. *Lord's News and Stories* (2021).

14. Hasbro. Mr. Potato Head Brand Update. *Hasbro Newsroom* (2021).

15. Tudeau, J. Townhall at MacEwan University, Edmonton. (2018).

16. Greer, G. *The Whole Woman*. (Black Swan, 1999).

17. Mulhuish, R. Cardiff University: Do not host Germaine Greer. *Change.org* (2015).

18. Greer, G. Women and Power: The Lessons of the 20th Century (lecture at Cardiff University). (2015).

19. Sommer, M., Kamowa, V. & Mahon, T. Opinion: Creating a more equal post-COVID-19 world for people who menstruate. *Devex* (2020).

20. US Quidditch and Major League Quidditch. USQ, MLQ Pursue Name Change for Quidditch. (2021).

21. Hachette UK. Statement on J. K. Rowling. (2020).

Chapter 2: Racial Justice

1. Segal, R. *The Black Diaspora: Five Centuries of the Black Experience Outside Africa*. (Farrar, Straus and Giroux, 1995).

2. Steckel, R. Analysis of Evidence from Plantation Records, *Social Science History*. **3** (3/4), 86-114 (Cambridge University Press, 1979).

3. Corruccini, R., Handler, J., et al., Osteology of a slave burial

population from Barbados West Indies, Am J Phys Anthropol., **59** (4), 443-59 (1982).

4. Cobbett, W. Debate on Mr. Wilberforce's Resolutions respecting the Slave Trade. in *The Parliamentary History of England. From the Norman Conquest in 1066 to the year 1803* (T. Curson Hansard, 1806).

5. Parks, R. *Rosa Parks: My Story.* (Puffin, 1992).

6. *Browder v Gayle.* (1956).

7. Branch, T. *Parting the Waters – America in the King Years 1954-63.* (Simon & Schuster Inc., 1988).

8. King, M. L. (Jr). I Have a Dream. (1963).

9. Eddo-Lodge, R. *Why I'm No Longer Talking to White People About Race.* (Bloomsbury Publishing, 2017).

10. Diangelo, R. *White Fragility – Why It's So Hard for White People to Talk About Racism.* (Penguin Random House, 2018).

11. Applebaum, B. Critical Whiteness Studies. in *Oxford Research Encyclopedia* (2016).

12. Murray, D. *The Madness of Crowds: Gender, Race and Identity.* (Bloomsbury Continuim, 2019).

13. *Fisher v University of Texas.* (2013).

14. *Students for Fair Admissions Inc. v President & Fellows of Harvard College.* (2014).

15. Quillian, L. Does Unconscious Racism Exist? *Soc. Psychol. Q.* **71**, 6–11 (2008).

16. Project Implicit. Implicit Association Tests Website. (2011).

17. Behavioural Insights Team. Unconscious bias and diversity training-what the evidence says. *Government Equalities Office* (2020).

18. Lopez, J. Unconscious Bias Training – Statement. *UK Parliment* (2020).

19. Kirkland, R. & Bohnet, I. Focusing on what works for workplace diversity. *McKinsey & Company* (2017).

20. Lett, E., Asabor, E. N., Corbin, T. & Boatright, D. Racial inequity in fatal US police shootings, 2015–2020. *J. Epidemiol. Community Health* **0**, (2020).

21. Buchanan, L., Bui, Q. & Patel, J. Black Lives Matter May be the Largest Movement in U.S. History. *New York Times* (2020).
22. ACLED. Demonstrations and Political Violence in Amercia: New Data for Summer 2020. (2020).
23. Kingson, J. Exclusive: $1 billion-plus riot damage is most expensive in insurance history. *Axios* (2020).
24. *R. v Graham & Ors.* (2022).
25. Kaepernick, C. Interview with ESPN. (2016).
26. Patel, P. Interview with Darren McCaffrey. *GB News* (2021).

Chapter 3: Gay Pride

1. American Psychiatric Association. *Diagnostic and Statistical Manual of Mental Disorders (1st Edition)*. (1952).
2. *R. v Turing.* (1952).
3. Leitsch, D. Mattachine Society Summer Newsletter. (1969).
4. Milk, H. The Hope Speech. (1978).
5. Stonewall. About Us. (2017).
6. *Sutherland v United Kingdom* (1997).
7. *Sexual Offences (Amendment) Act.* (2000).
8. *Adoption and Children Act.* (2002).
9. *Sexual Offences Act.* (2003).
10. *Civil Partnership Act.* (2004).
11. *Marriage (Same Sex Couples) Act.* (2013).
12. Hart, A. A Manifesto Club Report: Leave Those Kids Alone – How Official Hate Speech Regulation Interferes in School Life. *Manifesto Club* (2011).
13. Morgan, N. Exclusive: Nicky Morgan would 'probably' vote for equal marriage today. *Interview with Pink News* (2014).
14. Morgan, N. Interview with BBC Radio 4's Today Programme. (2015).
15. Bloom, D. Homophobic pupils could be extremists, says Tory Nicky Morgan – who voted against gay marriage. *The Mirror* (2015).
16. Department of Education. Relationships Education,

Relationships and Sex Education (RSE) and Health Education. (2019).

17. Stonewall. 2019: Statutory Relationships and Sex Education – a big step forward. (2019).

18. LittleJohn, R. 'Please don't pretend two dads is the new normal': Richard Littlejohn says children benefit most from being raised by a man and woman. *The Daily Mail.* (2018)

19. Duffy, N. Daily Mail columnist Richard Littlejohn attacks Tom Daley, gay parents: 'Pass the sick bag.' *Pink News.* (2018).

20. *Lee v Ashers Baking Co Ltd.* (2015).

21. *Lee v Ashers Baking Co Ltd.* (2016).

22. ECHR. Gay-Marriage-Case Declared Inadmissable, Press Release Issued by the Registrar of the Court. (2022).

23. Demianyk, G. Tim Farron Interview On Channel 4 News Sees Lib Dem Leader Branded An 'Absolute Disgrace.' *Huffington Post* (2017).

24. Farron, T. Tim Farron's Resignation Speech. (2017).

25. Cuthbertson, S. Cluck Off–No Chick Fil A in Scotland. *Change.org* (2019).

26. Valle, G. Del. Chick-fil-A's many controversies, explained. *Vox* (2019).

27. Cain, A. The Salvation Army urges the public to stop spreading 'misinformation' after Chick-fil-A cuts funding. *Business Insider* (2019).

28. Stonewall. Come Out For Trans Equality. (2019).

29. Parris, M. Stonewall should stay out of trans rights war. *The Times* (2021).

30. Hellen, N. 'Anti-women' trans policy may split Stonewall. *The Times* (2019).

31. Swerling, G. Trans dispute prompts new gay faction to break with Stonewall. *The Telegraph* (2019).

32. LCTR. Pledges for Labour Party members. (2020).

33. Gibbons, K. Gay groups clash over 'homophobic policies.' *The Times* (2019).

Chapter 4: Trans Rights

1. National Center for Transgender Equality. Frequently Asked Questions about Transgender People. (2016).

2. Government Equalities Office. *Trans People in the UK*. (2018).

3. Jorgensen, C. *Christine Jorgensen: A Personal Autobiography*. (Paul S. Eriksson, Inc., 1967).

4. King, D. & Ekins, R. Pioneers of Transgendering: The Life and Work of Virginia Prince. *GENDYS 2k, Sixth Int. Gend. Dysphoria Conf.* (2000).

5. *Corbett v Corbett*. (1970).

6. Feinberg, L. Trans Gender Liberation – A Movement Whose Time Has Come. (1992).

7. *Richards v United States Tennis Association*. (1977).

8. *Goodwin v United Kingdom*. (2002).

9. WHO. *International Statistical Classification of Diseases and Related Health Problems (ICD – 11)*. (2019).

10. Jenner, B. Interview with Diane Sawyer on *20/20*. *ABC News* (2015).

11. Sommer, M., Kamowa, V. & Mahon, T. Opinion: Creating a more equal post-COVID-19 world for people who menstruate. *Devex* (2020).

12. Brighton and Sussex University Hospitals. Gender Inclusive Language in Perinatal Services: Mission Statement and Rationale. (2021).

13. Davis, S. Periods on display. *Lancet* **398**, 1124–1125 (2021).

14. Horton, R. A statement from Richard Horton, Editor-in-Chief, The Lancet. (2021).

15. Gender Identity Development Service. Referrals to GIDS, financial years 2010-11 to 2020-21. (2021).

16. Brighton and Hove City Council. *Dorothy Stringer School Equality and Information Report*. (2018).

17. Scottish Government. Supporting Transgender Pupils in Schools – Guidance for Scottish Schools. (2021).

18. Erdol, T. *Practicing Gender Pedagogy: The Case of Egalia* Journal of Qualitative Research in Education. **7**(4) (2019).

19. Heyer, W. I Was a Transgender Woman. *Public Discourse J. Witherspoon Inst.* (2015).

20. Bell, K. Keira Bell: My Story. *Persuasion* (2021).

21. Bell v Tavistock and Portman NHS Foundation Trust. (2020).

22. Bell v Tavistock and Portman NHS Foundation Trust. (2021).

23. Mermaids. Mermaids statement on the Bell v Tavistock appeal. (2021).

24. Cass, H. The Cass Review – Independent review of gender identity services for children and young people: Interim report. (2022).

25. Wilchins, R. A. In Your Face: Political Activism Against Gender Oppression. (1995).

26. Nonbinary & Intersex Recognition Project. Our Movement. (2020).

27. Royal College of General Practitioners. The role of the GP in caring for gender-questioning and transgender patients: RCGP Position Statement. (2019).

28. Stonewall. List of LGBTQ+ terms – Trans (2017).

29. BBC Teach. Identity: Understanding Sexual and Gender Identities. (2019).

30. Gibson, N. Should There Be a Limit to Gender Identities? – interview on Good Morning Britain. (2019).

31. BBC. BBC Teach website, January 2021. *Contact the BBC* (2021).

Chapter 5: The Grand Narrative of Identity Politics

1. Pratchett, T. *I Shall Wear Midnight.* (Doubleday, 2010).

2. R. Bellah, et al. *Habits of the Heart: Individualism and Commitment in American Life.* (University of California Press, 1996).

3. Rousseau, J.-J. *Discourse on the Arts and Sciences.* (Translated by Victor Gourevitch, Cambridge: Cambridge University Press, 1750).

4. Rousseau, J.-J. *Emile; Or On Education.* (Translated by Allan Bloom, New York: Basic Books, 1763).

5. Rousseau, J.-J. *The Social Contract: or, Principles of Political Law.* (Peter Eckler Publisher, 1893).

6. Taylor, C. *Source of Self: The Making of the Modern Identity.* (Harvard University Press, 1989).

7. Trueman, C. *The Rise and Triumph of the Modern Self – Cultural Amnesia, Expressive Individualism, and the Road to Sexual Revolution.* (Crossway, 2020).

8. Scottish Government. Supporting Transgender Pupils in Schools: Guidance for Scottish Schools. (2021).

9. Marx, K. & Engels, F. *Manifesto of the Communist Party.* (Floating Press 2008, 1848).

10. Lyotard, J.-F. *The Postmodern Condition: A Report on Knowledge.* (Translated by Geoff Bennington and Brian Massumis, Minneapolis: University of Minnesota Press, 1979).

11. Holland, T. *Dominion: The Making of the Western Mind.* (Little Brown, 2019).

12. Nietzsche, F. *The Gay Science: with a prelude in German rhymes and an appendix of songs.* (Translated by Josefine Nauckhoff, Cambridge: Cambridge University Press, 1882).

13. Murray, D. *The Madness of Crowds: Gender, Race and Identity.* (Bloomsbury Continuim, 2019).

14. Burton, T. I. *Strange Rites: New Religions for a Godless World.* (Public Affairs New York, 2020).

15. Castro, M. *Peaceful Coexistence: Reconciling Nondiscrimination Principles with Civil Liberties.* (US Commission on Civil Rights, 2016).

16. Mounstephen, P. *Bishop of Truro's Independent Review for the Foreign Secretary of FCO Support for Persecuted Christians.* (2019).

17. Lindsay, B. *We Need To Talk About Race: Understanding the Black Experience in White Majority Churches.* (SPCK Publishing, 2019).

Chapter 6: Mirror

1. Mirza, M. 'Head-to-Head.' *BBC's Daily Politics* (2014).
2. Murray, D. *The Madness of Crowds: Gender, Race and Identity.* (Bloomsbury Continuim, 2019).
3. Giuliani, R. Interview with Rudy Giuliani. *CBS Face the Nation* (2016).
4. McCarthy, G. Townhall with Garry McCarthy. *CNN* (2016).
5. Burnley FC. Statement on 'White Lives Matter' Banner. (2020).
6. Chaudhary, V. & Tingle, R. Burnley fan and his girlfriend are both sacked from their jobs after he chartered the plane that flew White Lives Matter banner over the Etihad stadium. *Mail Online* (2020).
7. LCTR. Pledges for Labour Party members. (2020).
8. Gibbons, K. Gay groups clash over 'homophobic policies.' *The Times* (2019).
9. Fukuyama, F. *Identity: Contemporary Identity Politics and the Struggle for Recognition.* (Profile Books, 2019).
10. Nortey, J. Most White Amricans who regularly attend worship services voted for Trump in 2020. *Pew Research Center* (2021).
11. MacArthur, J. Interview in Falkrik Podcast 31: Church is Essential (2020).
12. MacArthur, J. Sermon at Grace Community Church. (2020).
13. Southern Baptist Convention. Resolution on Disney Company policy. *SBC Resolutions* (1996).
14. Pew Research Centre. Political Polarization in the American Public- How Increasing Ideological Uniformity and Partisan Antipathy Affect Politics, Compromise and Everyday Life. (2014).
15. ACLED. US Crisis Monitor. (2020).
16. Lewis, C. S. *Mere Christianity.* (HarperCollins, 1942).

Chapter 7: Argue

1. Lennox, J. & Dawkins, R. *The God Delusion Debate*. Fixed Point Foundation (2007).

2. Dawkins, R. *The God Delusion*. (Transworld Publishers, 2006).

3. Mulhuish, R. Cardiff University: Do not host Germaine Greer. *Change.org* (2015).

4. Greer, G. Interview on BBC's Newsnight. (2015).

5. Roche, N. Eliminate Dr. Kenneth Zucker and His Practice of Transgender 'Reparative Therapy.' *Change.org* (2015).

6. Ontario. *Affirming Sexual Orientation and Gender Identity Act*. Bill 77 (2015).

7. Paterson, T. As trans issues become mainstream, question of how to address variant gender expression comes to forefront. *National Post* (2015).

8. CAMH. *Summary of the External Review of the CAMH Gender Identity Clinic of the Child, Youth & Family Services*. (2016).

9. Ubelacker, S. CAMH to 'wind down' controversial gender identity clinic services. *The Canadian Press* (2015).

10. Chick-fil-A. Chick-fil-A's Closed-on-Sunday Policy. *Press Release* (2019).

11. Cuthbertson, S. Cluck Off–No Chick Fil A in Scotland. *Change.org* (2019).

12. Dodd, L. 2020: The Year of Evangelism. *Premier Christianity* (2019).

13. Shimron, Y. Franklin Graham vows UK tour will go on after planned venues back out. *Religion News Service* (2020).

14. R *(on the application of Ngole) v University of Sheffield*. (2017).

15. R *(on the application of Ngole) v University of Sheffield*. (2019).

16. Felix Ngole Case. *Christian Concern* (2019).

17. Orwell, G. The Freedom of the Press. *Times Literary Supplement* (1972).

18. Dawkins, R. Speech at the Edinburgh International Science Festival. *Quoted in The Independent* (1992).

Chapter 8: Ignore

1. Packer, J. I. When Billy Took Britain by Storm. *Christianity Today* (2018).

2. Peck, A. Billy Graham: His Impact on Britain. *Premier Christianity* (2001).

3. Larson, C. B. Why Graham's Preaching Worked. *Christianity Today* (2018).

4. Stott, J. Walking Together to Glory. *Christianity Today* (2018).

5. Tice, R. *Honest Evangelism: How to talk about Jesus when it's tough (with Carl Laferton)*. (The Good Book Company, 2015).

6. Chan, S. *Evangelism in a Skeptical World: How to Make the Unbelievable News about Jesus More Believable*. (Zondervan, 2018).

7. Gov.uk. UK Population by Ethnicity: Population of England and Wales. *Ethnicity Facts and Figures* (2018).

8. ONS. Sexual orientation, UK: 2019. *Annual Population Survey* (2019).

9. Government Equalities Office. *Trans People in the UK*. (2018).

10. The Church of England. *Living in Love & Faith: Christian teaching and learning about identity, sexuality, relationships and marriage*. (Church House Publishing, 2020).

Chapter 9: The Power of the Narrative

1. Walker, R., Glenn, J. *Significant Objects…and how they got that way*. (2009).

2. Simmons, A. *Whoever Tells the Best Story Wins: How to use your own stories to communicate with power and impact*. (American Management Association, 2015).

3. Nye, J. *Bound To Lead: The Changing Nature Of American Power*. (Basic Books, 1990).

4. Harrison, G. *A Better Story: God, Sex & Human Flourishing*. (Inter-Varsity Press, 2017).

5. Chan, S. *Evangelism in a Skeptical World: How to Make the Unbelievable News about Jesus More Believable*. (Zondervan, 2018).

6. Holland, T. *Dominion: The Making of the Western Mind*. (Little Brown, 2019).

Chapter 10: Have You Heard The One About...?

1. Jefferson, T., Adams, J., Franklin, B., Sherman, R. & Livingston, R. *The US Declaration of Independence.* (1776).

2. Lett, E., Asabor, E. N., Corbin, T. & Boatright, D. Racial inequity in fatal US police shootings, 2015–2020. *J. Epidemiol. Community Health* **0**, (2020).

4. Aristole. *Politics* (Translated by B. Jowett). (c. 330 BC).

5. Harari, Y. N. *Sapiens: A Brief History of Humankind.* (Vintage, 2015).

6. Wyatt, J. *Matters of Life and Death: Human Dilemmas in the Light of the Christian Faith.* (Inter-Varsity Press, 2009).

7. Holland, T. *Dominion: The Making of the Western Mind.* (Little Brown, 2019).

8. Quillian, L. Does Unconscious Racism Exist? *Soc. Psychol. Q.* **71**, 6–11 (2008).

9. Behavioural Insights Team. Unconscious bias and diversity training-what the evidence says. *Government Equalities Office* (2020).

10. Solzhenitsyn, A. *The Gulag Archipelago* (English Version). (Penguin, 1974).

11. Tice, R. & Cooper, B. *Christianity Explored.* (The Good Book Company, 2002).

12. Bell v Tavistock and Portman NHS Foundation Trust. (2021).

13. Bell v Tavistock and Portman NHS Foundation Trust. (2020).

14. Mermaids. *Mermaids Statement on the Bell v Tavistock Appeal* (2021).

15. Erdol, T. *Practicing Gender Pedagogy: The Case of Egalia* Journal of Qualitative Research in Education. **7**(4) (2019).

16. Gibbons, K. Gay groups clash over 'homophobic policies.' *The Times* (2019).

17. *Lee v Ashers Baking Co Ltd.* (2015).

18. *Lee v Ashers Baking Co Ltd.* (2016).

19. Harrison, G. *A Better Story: God, Sex & Human Flourishing.* (Inter-Varsity Press, 2017).

20. Stonewall. *About Us* (2017).21. Feinberg, L. Trans Gender Liberation: A Movement Whose Time Has Come. (1992).

22. Scottish Government. Supporting Transgender Pupils in Schools: Guidance for Scottish Schools. (2021).

23. Brighton and Sussex University Hospitals. Gender Inclusive Language in Perinatal Services: Mission Statement and Rationale. (2021).

24. Davis, S. Periods on display. *Lancet* **398**, 1124–1125 (2021).

25. Bell, K. Keira Bell: My Story. *Persuasion* (2021).

26. Heyer, W. I Was a Transgender Woman. *Public Discourse J. Witherspoon Inst.* (2015).

27. Lamb, J. *Ephesians 1:3-14: Saved By The Triune God*, Sermon at the Keswick Convention (2013).

28. Roberts, V. *Transgender.* (The Good Book Company, 2016).

29. Hart, A. A Manifesto Club Report: Leave Those Kids Alone. *Manifesto Club* (2011).

30. Dawkins, R. *River Out Of Eden: A Darwinian View of Life.* (Phoenix, 2001).

31. Huxley, T. H. *Evolution and Ethics: Collected Essays Volume IX.* (Macmillan and co., 1894).

Chapter 11: Speaking the Language of the Culture

1. Georges, J. *The 3D Gospel: Ministry in Guilt, Shame, and Fear Cultures.* (Time Press, 2017).

2. The Lausanne Movement. The Lausanne Covenant. (2009).

3. Roberts, V. Endorsement of The Cross of Christ, in *The Cross of Christ, Stott J. (20th Anniversary Edition)* (Inter-Varsity Press, 2006).

4. Stott, J. *The Cross of Christ.* (Inter-Varsity Press, 1986).

5. Jensen, P. & Payne, T. Two Ways to Live. *Matthias Media* (2021).

6. Bright, B. *Have You Heard of the Four Spiritual Laws?* (Bright Media Foundation and Campus Crusade for Christ, 2007).

7. Alpha. Episode 3: Why Did Jesus Die? *Alpha Film Series* (2019).

8. Tice, R. & Cooper, B. *Christianity Explored*. (The Good Book Company, 2002).

Chapter 12: Living Redemptively

1. Wright, C. *The Mission of God's People: A Biblical Theology of the Church's Mission*. (Zondervan, 2010).

2. Wenham, G. *The Book of Leviticus: New International Commentary on the Old Testament*. (Wm. B. Eerdmans Publishing, 1979).

4. Lewis, C. S. *The Weight of Glory and Other Addresses*. (William Collins, 1941).

5. Wyatt, J. *Matters of Life and Death: Human Dilemmas in the Light of the Christian Faith*. (Inter-Varsity Press, 2009).

6. Temple, W. *Christianity and Social Order*, 1976 Edition. (Shepheard-Walwyn Publishers, 1976).

7. Silverman, B. *Modern Slavery: an application of Multiple Systems Estimation*. (2014).

8. Ministry of Housing Communities and Local Government. *Rough sleeping snapshot in England: Autumn 2020*. (2020).

9. Cribb, J., Waters, T., Wernham, T. & Xu, X. Living standards, poverty and inequality in the UK: 2021. *IFS Rep. R194* (2021).

10. Unicef. Unicef UK Statement on Funding of UK Food Programmes (2020).

11. The Children and Social Care Secretariat. Adoption and Special Guardianship Leadership Board. (2021).

12. Wachtler, B. *et al.* Socioeconomic inequalities and COVID-19: A review of the current international literature. *J. Heal. Monit.* **5**, 3–17 (2020).

13. Whitehead, M., Taylor-Robinson, D. & Barr, B. Poverty, health, and COVID-19. *Br. Med. J.* **372**, 1–2 (2021).

14. Keller, T. *Generous Justice: How God's Grace Makes Us Just*. (Hodder & Stoughton, 2010).

15. Greene, M. *Fruitfulness on the Frontline: Making a Difference Where You Are*. (Inter-Varsity Press, 2014).

16. Tertullian, Q. *Apology Chapter 39 (translated by S. Thelwall)*. (179AD).

17. Stark, R. *The Rise of Christianity: How the Obscure, Marginal Jesus Movement Became the Dominant Religious Force in the Western World in a Few Centuries.* (Princeton University Press, 1996).

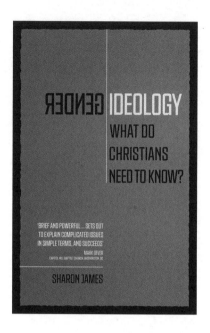

Gender Ideology
What Do Christians Need to Know?
Sharon James

- Equipping Christians to deal with transgenderism
- Defines and explains the subject
- Rebuts issues with the Christian worldview

The world has embraced the idea that gender is something
that can be decided by individuals. As Christians encounter
colleagues, friends and family members who identify as a gender
other than the one they were born, we need to be informed
and equipped with knowledge about what the issues are, what
different terms mean and what the Bible has to say about these
things. While we walk the line between loving our neighbour
and not buying into the world's lies, Sharon James helps us in
this informative and practical guide.

ISBN: 978-1-5271-0481-5

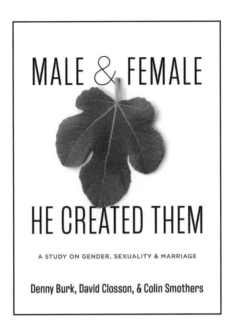

MALE & FEMALE

HE CREATED THEM

A STUDY ON GENDER, SEXUALITY & MARRIAGE

Denny Burk, David Closson, & Colin Smothers

Male and Female He Created Them
A Study on Gender, Sexuality, & Marriage
Denny Burk, Colin Smothers and David Closson

- Accessible curriculum for average church–goer
- Designed for group settings
- Includes journaling pages and conversation guides

Male & Female He Created Them is a study on gender, sexuality, and marriage. It presents a biblical vision for contested issues such as homosexuality, transgenderism, and marriage. By the completion of this book, readers will have a better grasp on the Bible's teaching about our identities as male and female, created in the image of God, and know how to apply Scripture to these issues in their ministries at church, home, and work.

ISBN: 978-1-5271-0974-2

Christian Focus Publications

Our mission statement –

STAYING FAITHFUL

In dependence upon God we seek to impact the world through literature faithful to His infallible Word, the Bible. Our aim is to ensure that the Lord Jesus Christ is presented as the only hope to obtain forgiveness of sin, live a useful life and look forward to heaven with Him.

Our books are published in four imprints:

CHRISTIAN FOCUS

Popular works including biographies, commentaries, basic doctrine and Christian living.

CHRISTIAN HERITAGE

Books representing some of the best material from the rich heritage of the church.

MENTOR

Books written at a level suitable for Bible College and seminary students, pastors, and other serious readers. The imprint includes commentaries, doctrinal studies, examination of current issues and church history.

CF4•K

Children's books for quality Bible teaching and for all age groups: Sunday school curriculum, puzzle and activity books; personal and family devotional titles, biographies and inspirational stories – because you are never too young to know Jesus!

Christian Focus Publications Ltd,
Geanies House, Fearn, Ross-shire,
IV20 1TW, Scotland, United Kingdom.
www.christianfocus.com